GAY CITY:
VOLUME ONE

EDITED BY VINCENT KOVAR, MICHAEL LEHMAN,
MALCOLM SMITH, JEFF CRANDALL AND J.A. DEVEAUX

www.GayCity.Org

Gay City: Volume One
Edited by Vincent Kovar
All rights reserved.

Published by Gay City Health Project:
511 East Pike Street
Seattle, WA 98122

ISBN: 978-0-6151-9240-6

Published with Kind Support From:

A Special Thank You to Our Sponsors

Justine Vick
▼

Jim Simmons & Mark Ketter
▼

Daniel Nye
▼

Jeffrey Maxwell
www.maxwell-law.com
▼

Julia Lowther
Flying Fox Jewelry
▼

Michael Lehman
www.moseattle.com
▼

Jefferson Coulter
www.axioslaw.com
▼

Jonathan Bowman
www.bowman4law.com
▼

Table of Contents

Introduction

BY VINCENT KOVAR

The first question everyone asks is, "why another gay anthology?" As a community, few of us are still reading gay-themed writing or patronizing the galleries and graphic novels created for gay audiences.

In the late eighties and early nineties, discussions in artistic circles focused on concerns that gay works were becoming too specialized towards a "niche" audience. Mainstream publishers dismissed queer creations as overly introspective, self-indulgent and of too low quality to compete in the larger marketplace. Even inside our own community a greater value has been placed on assimilation. Much of ourselves and our art has been jammed into the narrow tyranny of the term "straight acting," and our role as dynamic "outsiders" has faded away. So do we need another gay anthology?

We have made massive strides in both societal and legal acceptance, but have we reached a place of true liberation or have we become merely legitimate? Fiction, poetry, art and photography are not just products of individual imaginations but are part of the conversation our community is having with itself. If we want the global community to listen to us, perhaps we need to first listen to ourselves. We need to continue this artistic conversation and we need more gay anthologies.

We have endured and overcome, evolved and emerged, not to a specific destination but to the place where we are obliged to ask anew, "who are we now?" Included here are several answers to that question by both established and emerging artists. Here are author Tom Spanbauer's "Mr. Energy", written during the dark dawn of AIDS, alongside "Ethan Green" creator, Eric Orner's visual chronicle, "25 Years, 25 Fears." Inside you'll find an excerpt from syndicated columnist Michael Thomas Ford's novel "Full Circle", eight pieces from the award winning poet Peter Pereira, and groundbreaking works from artist, Donna Barr, plus many others.

Some would say that everything about "coming out" has been written; that everything about AIDS, gay relationships, religious conflict, exclusion and grief has already been "done." This slim anthology refutes that. We are our creations, and we still have much to say.

A BIRTHDAY VALENTINE: *ALTHEA ROSEA*

BY JEFFERY BEAM

Jeffery Beam's The Beautiful Tendons: Uncollected Queer Poems 1969 – 2007 is due June 2008 from White Crane Books/Lethe Press. His award-winning works include Visions of Dame Kind, An Elizabethan Bestiary, Gospel Earth, and The Fountain. The CD, What We Have Lost, was a 2003 Audie Award finalist. Beam, of Hillsborough, NC, is poetry editor of the print and online journal, Oyster Boy Review and a botanical librarian at UNC-Chapel Hill. www.unc.edu/~jeffbeam/index.html

▼

A Birthday Valentine: *Althea Rosea*

By Jeffrey Beam

For Stanley, April 4 & 5, 1992

Would that in this
                    early April of our births,
                                    the hollyhock, out-
landish rose of the Crusaders,
                    might guard the garden walk,
                                    in bloom.
Too early for that, but
                    not for the curled mound
                                    of rich green leaves
precious as their Chinese
                    and Indian origins.
                                    While the bees sleep
so
                    do these flowers.

Love comes out
                    of nowhere, or anywhere,
                                    or every,
and so,
                    like these mallows,
                                    warm underground
through Winter's wet mess and slump:
                    my love always.
                                    For summer hides
continually in the leaves,
                    and at once,
                                    when the sun calls,
opens pink and
                    singular on the stiff
                                    stalk.

MR. ENERGY

BY TOM SPANBAUER

Tom Spanbauer was born in Pocatello, Idaho, in a trunk in the Princess Theater. He attended High School in Pocatello, then went on to get his BA in English from Idaho State. In 1986, he received his MFA in Fiction at Columbia University. His novels include, Faraway Places-- newly released with Hawthorne Books--, The Man Who Fell In Love With The Moon, In The City of Shy Hunters, and Now Is The Hour. He lives in Portland, Oregon.

▼

Mr. Energy

By Tom Spanbauer

We gave him Mr. Energy for his birthday. He was thirty-nine and Neil Coussins, Cue Ball Marchetta, Anthony Parker, Howard Jones, and Ruby Prestigiacomo and me, we all got together and got Joe Mr. Energy for the night. It was a surprise and cost us each twenty-five dollars.

I didn't know whether or not to do it. It wasn't the twenty-five dollars. It was morality. But that's a bad word to use here, *morality*. Whenever I hear that word, *morality*, I think of an old Holy Cross nun with pucker lines around her lips. And it wasn't moral that way or immoral that way. It was just a feeling I had, the way you feel when you see a snake, suddenly there and awful.

But in the end, as it turned out, I finally decided to go ahead anyway, with getting Joe Mr. Energy for the night for twenty-five dollars. I hardly knew those guys but they were good friends of Joe; he had talked about them a lot and about the Phoenix a lot, and starting out with somebody new, I didn't want them to get the wrong idea about me, about me and Joe, you understand, and besides, those guys all said what a great dancer Mr. Energy was, so I finally said what the hell and went ahead.

I ended up going to the Phoenix twice, the first time was with Joe that night of his birthday, and the second time I went alone. The first time was when Joe introduced me to Neil, Cue Ball, Anthony, Howard, and Ruby. I had spoken to each one of those guys on the telephone at different times during that week before Joe's birthday concerning Joe's gift; how it was going to be delivered, what time at the Phoenix Joe was going to receive it, how it was going to be presented and so forth.

The *Grand Opening* is the way each of them had put it, on the telephone, and then laughed, each of them the same way, as if they had all been together one night planning the surprise, when one of them, probably Cue Ball or Ruby-they were the two characters in the bunch-came up with *The Grand Opening* and then they had all laughed hard, the way friends do.

After all that talking on the telephone with those guys, I was looking forward to Joe's birthday night at the Phoenix for a couple of reasons; I wanted to see Mr. Energy's Grand Opening and of course, I wanted to laugh too. I was looking forward to that night for those two reasons and others, but most of all, more than anything. I was looking forward to that night so that I could meet all those guys; Cue Ball, Howard, Anthony, and Ruby, and get to know them better, get to be friends.

I think it's true that you really can't tell much about people when you meet them in a bar. It's always the same; it's dark and the music's loud and everybody looks and acts the same. But, on the other hand, in a place like the Phoenix, you can tell a lot about a man. Just that a guy would go to the Phoenix says a lot about him.

I went back the second time because I wanted to watch Mr. Energy dance. The first time on Joe's birthday, I ended up leaving early and didn't get any of the things that I had gone to the Phoenix for: no dance, no grand opening, no nothing. I went back that second time because I couldn't forget what Cue Ball had told me on the telephone that week that we talked before Joe's birthday, that week that we all still talked to each other, and what Cue Ball had told me on the telephone, after he had told me about *The Grand Opening* and laughed was that Mr. Energy threw the best fuck in the fucking city, so, I'm sure you can understand that after hearing that, I was even more curious to see this Mr. Energy guy. But that's not the only reason why I went back. I went back because I wanted to watch Mr. Energy dance, and I went back to get a load at this best fuck in the fucking city, but also I went back because I wanted to watch those men, all those men standing around watching, I wanted to watch those men watch. And there was another reason, too.

Have you ever had a dream that you're naked and no one else is? It's that feeling that everyone, everyone who isn't you, knows instantly the thing about you that's important and wrong.

As soon as I walked into the Phoenix it was that feeling that you get when you walk into a dark hot place and it's hard to breathe and you can tell that all living eyes are on you. And as soon as I met those guys; Neil, Cue Ball, Howard, Anthony, and Ruby, in the flesh, it was that way and it was just that soon, too, that I could tell that Mr. Energy wasn't the only one who was *it* that night, and that there was more than one surprise ahead too.

Something wrong is what I felt, something not me and big out there in the dark and out of control is what I felt, watching.

But, as it turned out, I told myself it was just all in my head. I told myself to relax and enjoy the ride. And so I said what the hell, and ended up just going ahead.

So I went ahead, those guys behind me, Joe's friends and Joe, down the stairs, deeper into the Phoenix.

All of them, especially Cue Ball and Ruby, were enjoying themselves watching my body, but it was only because my body was a body that they hadn't seen before. They were enjoying themselves, watching my body, watching for what was important, for what was wrong, and as you can probably imagine, that wasn't helping matters out any. I really could have used one of Joe's downs, but I was afraid to ask Joe for a down because it would have meant that I was scared, which I was, and I knew that, but if I did that, asked for, say, a Quaalude, or a Tuilinol, for example, then it would have been a big unsmirked smirk, an uncovering of the underneath of things that would expose the wilderness down in there, the mass of wires taped and twisted together under the shiny hard surface of things.

I didn't know whether or not to do it, to go ahead and take that kind of risk, so, as it finally turned out, I ended up not asking Joe for a Quaalude, and instead I just told myself to relax and go ahead.

This is what the sign says: Safe Sex Rules: no kissing, no cocksucking, no fucking, no rimming ass. No body fluids exchanged. No cum exchanged. Remember: JO Clubs are jerk-off only.

You can read this sign as you take your clothes off at the door. You give your clothes to a guy behind the counter and he gives you a tag with a number on it that you can wear around your neck or pin to your shorts. I'm telling you this so that you'll know how to act if you ever decide to go to the Phoenix. Ten bucks at the door, all the beer, juice, or soda you want.

Most guys just wear their shorts, and, of course, their shoes and socks. I wore a T-shirt too, because I look better in a T-shirt. Neil, Anthony, Howard, and Joe all wore jockey shorts, Calvin Kleins, and no T-shirts, work boots and white socks. Cue Ball wore boxer shorts with hearts on them, no T-shirt and Nikes and no socks. Ruby's a cop and his jockey shorts had *Prestigiacomo* NYPD printed in black magic marker across the band in the back and he wore shiny black boots and regular issue black socks and black leather straps around his wrists with studs in them. I had bought a pair of Fruit of the Looms and a T-shirt, washed them so they didn't look new, but I didn't think about co-ordinating my shoes and socks. I had never thought of my underwear as an outfit. I was wearing black dress shoes and calf-high sup-hose.

It's the truth. I'm on my feet a lot and I was wearing calf high sup-hose. I was the only guy in that roomful of underwear who looked like he had just lost his pants.

Joe's friends were really enjoying themselves. I excused myself, went back to the clothes-check and gave the guy behind the counter my sup-hose. I have nice legs, and, after the elastic marks went away, the black dress shoes with no sup-hose didn't look that bad.

That first time, on Joe's birthday, I only stayed in the bar-part of the Phoenix. There was also a disco-part, and a catacombs part, too, that I went to the second time, but the first time I stayed only in the bar-part because Joe was there with his friends.

I should have gone to the disco-part. I should have ventured off on my own, explored, got out of there, got away from all that neon and industrial grey carpeting- you know you can assume viruses from industrial grey carpeting- but mostly I should have got away from those guys: Neil, Cue Ball, Howard, Anthony, Ruby, and Joe, but I was scared so I just stayed standing by those guys. If I would have gone to the disco-part I probably could have seen Mr. Energy dance that first time, and maybe could have avoided what happened. But I didn't.

I first knew for sure that something had gone haywire when I got back from getting my second beer. Joe and Cue Ball, Howard, Neil and Ruby were gone. Anthony was talking to a guy who was wearing long johns not buttoned in the back. When I came up to them, Anthony kind of turned his back to me and stepped closer to the guy in the long johns and laid his arms across the guy's shoulder. I should have taken my first step out of there right then, but instead, I stood alone, near Anthony, just behind him.

Out of the corner of my eye, I saw Joe and Ruby and Cue Ball talking to the bouncer. I saw Joe point his finger my way and all of them look over at me, but I pretended not to see them. I'm lucky I saw them pointing at me, otherwise I wouldn't have been prepared at all. The bouncer is this big guy with a hairy chest, of course, wearing a jock strap that looked more like a sling whose supports had given way from too much weight and thrust. In other words, underneath, he was hung like a horse.

The bouncer walked up behind me and told me that I was the most beautiful fucking man in the world and that I got him so fucking hot that he couldn't control himself and he put his cock in the crack of my ass, pulled down my shorts in the front and held my cock and balls, my penis-envy cock, my I wish it were bigger cock, my flaccid penis, in his hands, he held it. He walked around, facing me, pulled his horse cock out of the red pouch; it was getting harder and bigger, he came around to the front of me and held us both in his hands there, a mountain and a mole hill. He started jerking off and groaning and telling me I was too fucking hot to believe, and then he started rubbing himself against me. Men were gathering around. I thought: why don't they try and stop him. Then: this is a jerk-off club, I thought, this is what they do in a jerk-off club. Then I had the thought that I should remember something, something important that I should do or think; a stance, a motto-survival of the fittest or something-some way to remember that would help get me through this, through times like this, but then I thought that I couldn't protect myself, or act like I even needed to protect myself, because when it came right down to it, there wasn't anything to protect myself against, I mean, after all, the Phoenix *was* a jerk-off club. So I ended up just standing, trying to find the right facial expression, trying to hold the muscles in my body normally, as if this sort of thing happened to me all the time, and I didn't know what to do with my can of beer, and then the bouncer took the can from my hand and poured the beer over his cock. His cock did not retreat from the cold beer, and the cold beer made a sound as he pulled at his cock.

The bouncer was using my Budweiser as a lubricant.

Neil, Cue Ball, Anthony, Ruby, and Joe, and this guy in the long johns and others were laughing. I couldn't hear them laughing, though after a while, I couldn't see them either. All I was aware of was a switchboard of lights and wires flashing and sparking. *Launch window* were the first words that crossed my mind. I probably moved my lips to speak the words, *launch window*, and then I thought it was curious that I should think or say *launch window*, the time within which a rocket must be launched to accomplish its mission.

The bouncer pulled his knees together then and started a slow grind and the crowd stepped back. His cock got that hard way it gets when you're in the last stages, for one beat, two, three, and then, with a jerk, he turned and shot his load onto the floor, onto the industrial grey carpeting.

For a moment, for support, the bouncer put his forehead on my shoulder. Everything about me was hot, not horny hot, not gonad hot, but hot ridiculed, hot embarrassed. It got too hot in my head, too hot and somewhere along the line I had quit thinking, and I grabbed the bouncer by the back of his head by the hair and pulled his head back hard and made him look into my eyes. I looked into his eyes, into launch window, because the underneath comes out when you come, how things really are with you comes out in your eyes when you come, even his.

I kissed him.

I kissed him so that Neil, Cue Ball, Howard, Anthony, and Ruby would see, and Joe, and Long Johns and whoever else, would see.

I kissed him hard and long because I had seen him way down, see him in launch window, seen myself.

I closed my eyes then because I didn't want to see anymore, and finally, the bouncer pulled himself away and covered himself up with the red pouch.

"No kissing, man," he said. "It's against the rules."

For weeks after that first time, all I thought about was sup-hose. I tried to reinvent the evening as if I had worn regular black socks, white socks, different socks, different shoes, different evening altogether, but it came back to sup-hose. I had even bought a new outfit and practiced at home in front of the mirror. I had it down perfect, like it was my own: Calvin Klein shorts and T-shirt, work boots (brown), and all-cotton white socks. But I didn't go back. I thought constantly of going back to the Phoenix, but I didn't go back.

It was some time later, some months later that Anthony called.

"Anthony who?" I said.

"Anthony Parker," Anthony said.

"Oh," I said.

"You might remember me from the Phoenix," Anthony said. "I was friends with Joe, Neil, Howard, Cue Ball and Ruby."

"Oh yes," I said. "Of course," "Anthony Parker," I said.

"Joe died last night," Anthony said, "and Cue Ball and Ruby are sick. Both of them are in St. Vincent's."

I just hung up the telephone then. I don't think I even said anything. I just hung up the telephone. *The Grand Opening* is what I was thinking, and I felt like I was back in that dark hot place again, with that big thing out there and it was hard to breathe. *The Grand Opening* is what I was saying over and over, I picked up the telephone again and Anthony Parker was gone and I didn't know who else to call, and nobody was on the line, and there was only that telephone sound.

I get them mixed up now, the funerals, all of them Italian and on Staten Island. Actually, there are only two things worth mentioning about the funerals, two things I remember, I mean, that I'll never forget.

The first is a picture of the three of them; Joe, Cue Ball, and Ruby, on the Prestigiacomo's mantle, surrounded with carnations and roses; three boys in soccer drag, their arms about each other, male friends, mates, healthy young American boys. It was such a small photograph and such a big room.

And the second is not something I saw or heard. It was not something I thought. On the ferry back each time, after each funeral, it was a feeling: that which wasn't there got bigger than that which was, each time after each funeral that opening, a window inside you opened wider, sudden and awful, that thrust.

As it ended up, I finally just had to stop thinking about how things got so wrong so fast, had to stop thinking about the injustice of it all, of death, after a life like this just death, and so I said what the hell and just ended up going ahead.

There wasn't as many men there the second time. I stayed for a while in the bar-part. I went back to the bar three times for beers just to make sure that I had it all down right. Several guys came back around twice, one guy three times, but I ignored them. The bouncer was the same bouncer as the first time, same outfit, too. He pretended he didn't remember. I remembered, but didn't say anything or act in a way that remembered. He thought I had forgotten, too. Anthony wasn't there, neither was Neil, or Howard. I didn't see Long Johns, either.

In the disco-part, I settled back against the leather banquet and watched Mr. Energy dance. I watched the men watch him dance up there on the stage. He had one of those health club bodies that likes a fuss, and wore a T-shirt with Einstein on it and then peeled it off. When his dance was finished, I handed Einstein back up to Mr. Energy, along with a bottle of poppers and a note. I found him later in the catacombs-part with the bottle of poppers breaking a safe-sex rule, throwing the best fuck in the fucking city. I stood in the darkness, my heart pounding, and watched. I didn't say anything because I figure when your time's up you die.

Mr. Energy laid himself back on the bench and lifted his legs in the air and held them with his left forearm behind his knees. He spit onto the fingers of his right hand and rubbed the spit into that grand asshole of his and squirmed and spread his legs out. "Hurry up!" The bouncer will be back through any minute!" Mr. Energy said.

The other guy was busy trying to get a rubber onto his cock. His cock was not very large and curved up.

"Hurry!" Mr. Energy said.

The guy just stuck it in fast into Mr. Energy without a rubber and pumped hard for fifteen or twenty seconds, and then it was over.

They stayed that way for a while. And so did I. Then the guy pulled himself out and then pulled some money from his sock, his white L. L. Bean sock, and handed it to Mr. Energy.

He came home with me for fifty dollars. I was surprised. I had expected to pay more for Mr. Energy. He didn't remember Joe's birthday, or what happened on Joe's birthday, or Joe, or Cue Ball, or Ruby, Howard, Neil or Anthony.

Mr. Energy remembered me, though.

Mr. Energy laughed when he told me he remembered me because of my sup-hose and the bouncer jacking on me that first time.

I laughed too. It was funny this time, remembering myself standing in my sup-hose, and then after that, standing stiff as a Holy Cross nun, pucker lines around my lips, holding on for dear life to a can of Budweiser with that bouncer after me.

"Tell me what you want me to do," Mr. Energy said.

"I don't want you to do anything," I said.

"You just watch, then, other men fucking?" he asked, "I saw you watching in the catacombs."

"I like to do more than watch," I said. "But not tonight."

I knew that he thought that not tonight meant because of the epidemic we're having, which wasn't exactly the case, but what the hell, it's not important, who cares what he thinks, I thought. I was just very tired of the same old count down, tired of that same old snake in the grass, tired of just doing things, of just going ahead and doing things.

"Well, there's something I want," Mr. Energy said. He reached into his pocket and pulled out a roll of bills, and threw twenty-five out onto the bed sheet.

"I want you to kiss me," he said. "Kiss me like you kissed the bouncer."

GREEN MAN & PERVERTS

BY DONNA BARR

Donna Barr has been a ground-breaking author/artist of comic-books since 1986. Her Desert Peach was the first non-underground gay character in a regularly-published series; it addressed German/Jewish relationships and historical developments before Maus. Barr opened the field to female authors and artists by refusing to be contained in genre or gender, and doing end-runs around the male-oriented, piecework Eisner system. More: http://en.wikipedia.org/wiki/Donna_Barr

▼

Greenman

BY DONNA BARR

Perverts

By Donna Barr

PETER PEREIRA: EIGHT POEMS

BY PETER PEREIRA

Peter Pereira's poems have appeared in Poetry, Prairie Schooner, New England Review, Virginia Quarterly Review and in the 2007 Best American Poetry. His poetry has also been featured in the Seattle Times and Seattle Post Intelligencer, as well as on Garrison Keillor's The Writer's Almanac. His books include The Lost Twin (Grey Spider 2000), Saying the World (Copper Canyon, 2003), and What's Written on the Body, newly released by Copper Canyon in 2007. He is a family physician at High Point Community Clinic, and lives in Seattle with his partner Dean Allan.

▼

Celestial Navigation: Vermont - Seattle, 2003

BY PETER PEREIRA

Mid-Autumn, Johnson, Vermont,
I'm thinking of home and how
last summer you and I walked
to the hillside above Lake Washington,
watched Mars rise fiery and mandarin
in the southern sky — closest
the planet had been to earth
in sixty thousand years.

Now tonight, I'm on the other side
of the continent, missing you,
and there it is again — Mars rising
from the same spot in the sky, as if all
this distance between us were nothing —
making me feel small, our life
and love so fleeting, so persistent,
against the background of the fixed
stars, the wandering planets.

Gay Test

BY PETER PEREIRA

Look at your fingernails.
Do you make a fist or
splay your fingers like a fan?

Hold your arms out, palms up.
Do your elbows touch
before your wrists?

Now: Skip across the room.
Stand on one foot.

Say *boring.*
Say *fabulous.*

Have you ever ended a sentence
with a proposition?

When someone says "boa"
do you see a feather scarf,
or a large snake?

If a man on the bus touches your knee,
do you want to say, "Don't. Stop."
Or "Don't stop."

When someone yells
"Hey, faggot."
Do you look?

Interrogation

By Peter Pereira

Were you there?
Were you present when they
bound his hands, forced him to stand
three days, beat his feet
if he tried to lie down?

Were you there when they
covered his face with a gunny sack,
poured cold water over his head,
twisted both arms backwards,
suspended him by his wrists,
dislocated his shoulders?

Did you say anything
when they burned him
with their cigarettes, attached
electrodes to his privates,
brought in snarling dogs?

Did you watch as they took him
down and kneeled upon his chest,
broke several ribs without leaving a bruise,
covered his face in cellophane,
strapped him to a board?

Did you try to stop it
when they showed him
a photograph of his lover,
whispered that they had taken him
into custody, too?

Were you there?
Did you watch?
Did you say anything?
Did you try to stop it?
Did you protest?

Last Days

By Peter Pereira

A man sits on a tin bucket outside a church
waving a sign that says "Jesus Hates Gays."
He doesn't seem angry, just cold,
bored, as he picks a scab
from the side of his face.

I think of Satan in his innermost circle
of hell, remember that summer a park ranger
flicked off the lights down inside
Lewis & Clark Caverns, how we were
suspended there, feeling the earth's dank center,
damp drip, buried alive, that utter aloneness.

"Faggot," the man croaks, as
my partner and I approach. "Have you ever
looked it up?" he says. "It's a bundle
of sticks, a cigarette, something to be set on fire."
And as we pass: "Something to be tied
with string, held under water."

Such darkness in the middle of the day.
I remember when the ranger flicked on the lights,
how bright our faces seemed, as if
we were miners miraculously rescued
from a cave-in. And ready to return
to the earth's bright surface.

Mattering

By Peter Pereira

They say the universe is largely empty
space, that even the bits we're made of contain
mostly nothing. Yet this chair, this window

seem solid enough. And while you were away,
I felt your absence more acutely than if
you had just left the room — all the places

you weren't: kitchen table, basement sofa,
the soft flannel of work shirts draped
across the bed post. *What's the matter?*

you said, when I met you at the airport,
the weight of your arm in mine
so real, so material, it almost hurt.

It's as if my bones and blood could recall
every atom moving from your body to mine,
mine to yours, over the years so much traded

that each of us retains as much of the other
as of the self. Like the shape left on a cushion
or pillow. Form of a hand within a garden glove.

Imagine: aligned just right we could pass
completely through each other, emerge
unscathed, but not unchanged.

Pregnant Man

BY PETER PEREIRA

*— Another Person Lived Inside a Man for Nearly Four
Decades*

ABC News Aug. 23, 2006

He'd felt ashamed his whole life
about his belly so swollen he looked nine
months pregnant, could barely breathe.

Doctors thought a giant tumor,
decided to operate. But as they cut
gallons of fluid spilled out — and

they found a body inside.
A small leg, one arm, then some part of genitalia,
then part of a cranium covered with hair,

a half-formed creature with feet and
hands, fingernails that were quite long. As if
a monster had been born from his stomach.

One fetus wraps around and envelops the other
they said. *The one twin grows, the other feeds
off its host like a kind of parasite.*

No one suspected he carried another man
inside him. For 36 years it was his shame
and misery, people in the village

mercilessly teasing, saying he looked
fat as a woman great with child.
Ironically, they were half right.

Like a woman he gave birth
to a man. Like a man he was healed
by freeing the man trapped inside him.

Sebastian

By Peter Pereira

— patron saint of archers, athletes, soldiers, and gay men,
Sebastian is appealed to for protection against plagues.

Bound to a tree's
alabaster column

by ropes, loincloth falling
from muscular hips,

an anguished quivering
upward gaze upon his face.

Punctured in thigh
and throat. The wounds

upon his body
bleeding, feminine.

Drawn to this image
as a child,

even before I learned
his story, somehow

I understood —
it was not *arrows*,

but *eros*
that pierced him.

When Love Means Nothing

BY PETER PEREIRA

— for Mary S.

Because you heard I was good, and because
you refuse to play your husband —
he's accused you one time too many of
not trying — you've brought
your limp-wristed backhand
and spin serve to me, looking for a second.

Clearly, I'm not the first.
After ditching several of my floaters
into the net you bark, *Stroke it harder!*
I hit better against pace!

So I go for the lines, chip and approach,
angle a volley wide to your forehand, slam
your short lob into the corner. *This is great,*
you say, during a changeover.
Exactly what I'm wanting.

It's your idea to play points,
keep score. I balk, fearing a rout.
I don't mind losing, you insist,
toweling sweat from your forearms.
Only winners who apologize.

We're done in love and one.
Yet you've shown me the best
partner is not necessarily an equal
partner. That there's a certain pleasure
not only in winning, but
in being soundly beaten.

PHOTOGRAPHY

By Jan Stary

For Jan, photography is painting with light. Besides finding beauty in the unusual suspects in nature, his all-life passion for the art of dance has led him to explore the beauty of male physique. Jan has shown his art in different cities and galleries including Czech Republic, Poland, and USA. A former university professor, a translator for President Vaclav Havel, and a diplomat, Jan is a photographer residing in Seattle with his partner of 16 years, Mark Shimada.

▼

Ascension

BY JAN STARY

Entrapment

By Jan Stary

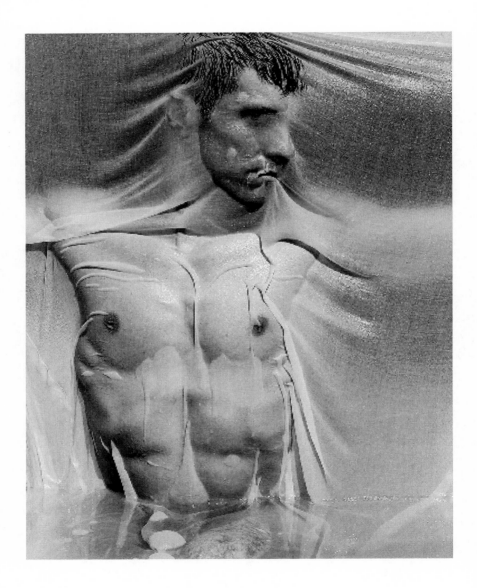

Oneness

BY JAN STARY

TO DREAM OF A LASTING LOVE

By Christopher Smith

Christopher Smith is a writer currently living in his native city of Houston, Texas. He is fiction editor for the online magazine iddie. He has never experienced the shape-shifting trials of his main character, but his literary tastes do undergo a similarly rapid and continual metamorphosis. As does his residence: he has lived in Houston, Chicago, and Seattle, and at present is contemplating New York. Gay City Volume 1 represents his first appearance in print.

▼

To Dream of a Lasting Love

By Christopher Smith

Two men lay in bed, tossed apart in their sleep. Only the morning sun, spilling over both, connected them. One began to stir, a faint smile playing across his lips. He rubbed his palms into his eyes, an action which somehow accentuated the two ruddy patches on his cheeks. He ran a hand through his black curly hair. Turned towards his companion, still buried deep in the blankets.

Something seemed odd. The bulk was heavier, taking up more space than he'd expect from the slender body he'd brought home. He reached over to stroke the hair. His eyes opened wider. What had been shoulder length and silky fine now felt short and thick. He pulled back the sheet. He took in a breath. The delicate dark-haired figure of the night before was now replaced by a sturdy looking bearded blonde. He searched his mind for the man's name...or at least the name of the man he had come home with: "Richard?"

Richard stirred beside him. "Yes?"

"What the hell!"

Richard's eyes snapped open. They were now blue. His hands flew to his face. He discovered the hawk nose where once an upturned English had been. He sat up, looked down at his torso. Sculptured, firm, a pattern of golden hair swept across the chest. He looked apologetic.

"I know. This happens."

"*What* happens?"

Richard gestured at his body. "This." The bass of his voice less from sleep than the greater depth of the new instrument. "Don't freak out, Michael. I'm still me. I don't want you to think I've changed."

A darker, strident red seeped into Michael's cheeks. "Get out. Get the fuck out of here. Now!"

At the last word, Richard leapt out of bed. He was larger than Michael now, and could easily have overpowered him, but instead rushed into his clothes. He turned as he stuck a leg into his pants. "Look, I just want you to understand. It's nothing serious."

"If you've given me some fucking disease!"

Richard wrapped his shirt around his body. "It's not like that--" But the words halted on his lips. It was useless. The look in Michael's eyes shut off any other communication between them. Richard rushed out the door, one shoe hanging from his toe, shirttail poking out through his zipper, his clothes not half fitting the form he now inhabited.

He turned back a final time at the bottom of the apartment steps. "Really, it's not what you think." But Michael stood in his doorway, implacable, waiting only to make sure the security gate shut firmly behind him.

Outside in the visitor's parking lot, Richard fell into his car. He sat for a moment, trying to catch his breath. Looking up at the rearview mirror, he caught the gaze of his new blue eyes. Then looked over towards the apartments where someone never wanted to see him again.

Well, not everyone can appreciate it.

He drove home in silence. A shower restored him somewhat, as he lathered and rinsed his new body. Afterwards, he examined himself in the full-length mirror.

"Pretty nice," he told himself.

That wasn't the half of it. He contemplated the evening ahead, considered the possibility it held. If the mornings could be nightmares, the evenings were dreams come true. For a while there, he'd gone through a rough patch, bent noses and wizened frames. It was impossible. He'd stayed home and watched television. But the last few weeks had produced a winning streak. And in this particular instance, he realized he struck gold to match the hair on his face.

He hit the gym that afternoon. The girl at the front desk looked up with a smile. He handed her his membership card. This was the tricky part. Yes, he had a membership, but he never resembled his driver's license. When the changes had first begun, he'd avoided the place. The first time he'd chanced it, they asked for picture i.d. He choked, insisting frantically that he had to get in, pulling out a crumpled twenty from his wallet and throwing it across the desk. When the desk clerk reached for the phone, he bolted.

This was before he'd discovered the amnesiac effect. People forgot him quickly, even within hours of meeting. No matter how intense the encounter--and Richard had given some men phenomenal sex--all memory of him was wiped clear within at most the space of a day. At least he knew he could go back to the gym.

"I.d.?"

He leaned on the counter, smiling into her eyes. "I realized just as I was getting here, I left my license at home." She evidenced some trouble swallowing. Held his card up to the electronic sensor, almost dropped it. Returned it to him, hand slightly shaking. "Have a good workout." *At least I've learned that much.*

He walked through the gym, men turning their heads as he passed. He'd been bigger. He'd been more powerful. But today he inhabited a body in perfect symmetry. Most of the looks were not rapacious. Some were. Two men caught sight of him and exchanged glances. He could find them in the sauna if he liked. *But it's not me they want. Not really.*

Today seemed a good day for biceps, chest and back. Yesterday, with his pale delicate body, he'd restricted himself to aerobics. To his surprise, he'd found he could push himself on the step-machine for over an hour at peak performance. He'd discovered once again he never should underestimate a body.

He found an empty bench press. He considered what weight to load. He could probably do 200. He slid under the bar and began his workout. The body felt good. The warmth from stretching the muscles soothing. Still, it was hard to tell if he was pushing too hard or going easy on himself. Always, there was a certain danger in chancing what he could hold.

Biceps. He picked up a pair of 50 pound dumbbells. Maybe it taught him a few things about adaptation to the new shell. Certainly it helped to psyche him up for the night. Concentrating on his form, he was concentrating on his future, granted the future of one night only.

Back. He shoved back with his feet, his legs sturdy, and began to row. He'd loaded the weights as high as he could. A powerful back. A very satisfying set. With his constantly changing shape, he never knew what his workouts accomplished. What was he maintaining? This body would be gone in the morning. Why bother at all? He went to the gym because he always went to the gym. Appearances to the contrary, he valued consistency.

At home that evening, he donned a plaid shirt and work boots. Practiced his gait so that he'd have the easygoing workingman bit down pat, and headed out. He knew exactly what he wanted, and by now had learned the means to get it.

It took a little searching, harder than usual. The bars were packed, and he wasn't finding what he wanted in the usual places. Men stepped in front of him, smiling, or called out a hello, striving to make eye contact.

He continued to walk, not wanting to be rude, nor overly concerned. In the early days, he'd been very careful about his response. Hours were wasted talking to men he had no interest in. But he had learned that people would hate him for the rejection, or themselves for the rejection, no matter how he treated them. If he tried to be nice, they would only accuse him of teasing or tormenting. He didn't have the time for that. He knew what he wanted. Specifically whom he wanted.

And finally, in a downtown sports bar, sitting at the counter, a look of sadness on his face, was the very man. He looked like he'd been hurt by life, hurt recently. Richard smiled to himself with satisfaction. *It's something*. The man looked like he needed to recover, and this was more satisfaction. *It's something I can do*. He pitched his voice as low and caressing as he could.

"Buy you a beer?"

The man looked up to say no, but when he saw Richard, he stopped himself. "Jack and coke. Thanks."

Richard turned to the bartender who, though busy with other customers, hopped to attention.

He ordered the man's drink, and a Miller Lite for himself. He turned back to the man. "Meeting friends?"

"No. Stopped in for a drink."

"Hope I'm not bothering you."

The man gave Richard a smile. "No."

"You look a little troubled."

"Tough day." He ran a hand through his black curly hair. Looked at a loss. "Strange."

"I'm sorry."

"No, it's okay." They took their drinks. The man's cheeks had seemed too pale at first, but whiskey brought back a ruddy patch to each. "I can't put my finger on it. It's like I woke up on the wrong side of the bed? Just something has been off." He smiled, but not the smile of happiness. "I really don't know what it is. Not a clue."

"I didn't introduce myself," Richard said, extending his hand. "Richard." The man took it. "Michael."

They exchanged small talk. After another drink, Richard returned to the subject of Michael's day. "Would it help to talk about it?"

"Oh, you don't have to…actually, I don't know what the trouble is. Or was. I was really upset this morning about something."

"What?"

Michael smiled, embarrassed. "That's just it. Damn if I know now. Something."

"Just getting worse, the longer you think about it?"

"Easier, actually. I was really angry about..." he made a hopeless gesture. "Then after a while it was more I was just kinda down. Now, I'm starting to feel silly about the whole thing." He paused. "Maybe talking with you makes it better."

Richard smiled.

"I think really I just woke up on the wrong side of the bed."

"Maybe you'll wake up on the right side tomorrow."

They looked at each other for a moment.

Suddenly, a group of Michael's friends rushed up, pulling at his arm.

"We didn't know you'd be out tonight."

"Good DJ."

"Come on, this is your song."

Michael only half resisted. He seemed clearly pleased to be adored by a small crowd in front of a man like Richard, and he let them drag him towards the dance floor. "I'll be right back," he said. "I promise."

The smile on Richard's face froze as he watched him leave. He knew the sort of trouble this brought. He looked at the clock on the wall, watched several minutes go by. He should see to this. But a perverse mood struck him, and he waited over half an hour.

He walked down to the dance floor. He scanned the crowd, finally spotted them, slipping around the notes echoing from the surround system. He tapped Michael on the shoulder. Michael turned, looked at him for a moment with a surprised, questioning smile, clearly not recognizing him. Then suddenly--"Richard!" He looked very embarrassed. "I'm sorry, I--I don't know what happened."

"I should be heading home."

"Don't go." He reached out. "I can't explain. I must have lost my mind. Hey, I owe you a drink, don't I? You bought me two." He placed a hand on Richard's shoulder, and propelled him back to the bar. "C'mon."

Richard allowed himself to be guided.

They had another drink. "It's funny you're being here tonight," Michael said. "I haven't really met a man like you. And today of all days."

Richard half stood playfully, as if to go.

Michael pulled him back. "No. You're good here." Richard pretended to struggle a moment. They were being ridiculous, they knew it, but it gave them the opportunity to touch each other.

"It was good you were here tonight." Michael said. He looked into Richard's face, then down at his glass. "They're making the drinks strong tonight." He examined Richard's hand lying on the counter. The red of the knuckles thrown into relief by the white fingers, visible even under the red-tint lights the bar employed to hide bad skin. He turned the hand over, placing it in his own. Red palm to match the knuckles. He felt the calluses, the rough surface that comes from day labor. He looked up. "Good. All of you, really."

Richard closed his hand over Michael's. They leaned into each other.

Back in Michael's bed, Richard held him as he slept. One of the laws he'd discovered was that he had to fall asleep before he could change. Usually Michael remembered him for a while after sex. He'd ball parked it at about ten hours or so, if he stayed the same. He could stay awake, and there would be a pleasant goodbye in the morning. The promise of a call. Though Michael would have forgotten him maybe before Richard even got home. Or he could go to sleep—and there was nothing more comforting than to sleep next to the man he loved. But the shock, the startled jolt when Michael would discover him the next day, was always as intense, as painful as if it were the first time. He never got used to it. Which was better? One choice shattered him, the other chipped slowly away at his soul.

When Michael opened his eyes the next morning, Richard was staring down at him, still the man of the night before. Michael nuzzled his head in the crook of Richard's arm. Richard ran his fingers through his curls.

"Sleep well?"

Michael smiled. "Hmm. You?"

"Perfect peace."

Michael pulled himself closer into the arms of this strong, gentle man. "This is nice." Richard was silent.

Michael sat up. "You know what? Let's spend the day together."

The smile on Richard's face was fading slightly. Circles had formed under his eyes. Still, Michael had never extended this invitation before. He tried to brush off his tiredness. "Sure. Sounds good." Michael leapt up, his energy restored during the night.

At a nearby restaurant, they scooped eggs into their mouths as their knees touched under the little wooden table. They went to the park where there was nothing to do, and they did nothing together. They walked along the lake. Richard bought Michael an ice crème cone. They stretched out on the grass.

"I teach. Grammar school," Michael said. "I don't tell men that right off. They look at me funny. It's not a Fortune 500 career."

"Do you like it?" Richard already knew the answer.

"Yeah. I mean, these kids. You're influencing them at the very start of their life. If they stay with us through grammar school, they'll have known me half as long as they've known their parents, they'll have known me for 50% of their life."

"I've never been a teacher," Richard said. "But I think I'd like to have kids." Michael sat up on his elbow when he heard this.

They wandered over to the museum, their hands entwined. They looked at dinosaur skeletons and butterflies. The afternoon wore on, and they wound up back at Michael's place, kissing, falling onto the bed.

Afterwards, as they lay there, Michael stroked Richard's beard. "You don't scratch at all. You look so tough. But you feel…" He stopped himself from saying more. "I'm tired again. We didn't get much rest. You want to take a nap?"

The day was dragging on Richard. He could feel the last of his energy slipping away, the pull into oblivion. He wanted this day to end with hope, to leave early, to kiss at the door with the promise of a call.

"I'm kinda beat. I don't think I got as much sleep as you."

"If you're worn out, you can't drive. It's dangerous." Michael tugged at his arm. "Come on, let's just lie here for a few hours. We could have dinner together after." His face held the look of wide-eyed innocence he might have picked up from the children in his class, pleading for longer recess.

"Okay."

They looked at each other, a half smile on both their faces, as if they each were about to say something, as if they could almost read it in each other's eyes. But neither said anything. Michael threw himself against Richard's chest, curling up into his body, and soon was fast asleep.

Sleep was pulling at Richard. As always, the same argument played in his mind. Should he leave now, while he still could? Let Michael wake up to remember…vaguely…for a few hours…? Or go to sleep and awake to Michael's confusion and hatred at Richard in his next form?

At some point I've got to run out of different bodies to change into, don't I? Would he be stuck in the last one, good or bad? Would the cycle start over? Or would he maybe just disappear altogether?

He shivered slightly, moved to disentangle himself and get away. But Michael, still asleep, pulled him back, a smile playing on his face, though his eyes remained firmly shut. *Why does he always want to hold me so close at this point? He'll shove me away tomorrow.*

Still, he was too tired to resist, and it felt so good. He kissed Michael softly on the lips, and eased down beside him. This was the most he could get, these few hours of security, wrapped tightly in his arms. These moments where it felt as if they would hold each other forever. He pulled Michael more snugly against him, and closed his eyes. *For all the trouble, I like it when we get to this moment. Just this right here. Drifting off with our arms around each other.* Soon Richard was unconscious, and breathing gently.

TWENTY FIVE YEARS, TWENTY FIVE FEARS

By Eric Orner

Eric Orner is a cartoonist and animation artist whose comics and graphic stories have appeared in Newsweek, The New Republic and McSweeney's. He's worked on a number of animated features including Disney's upcoming Tinker Bell movie. A feature film based on Eric's widely published comic strip, "The Mostly Unfabulous Social Life of Ethan Green" was released nationally in 2006. The comic strip has been anthologized in 4 books from St. Martin's Press.

▼

TWENTY FIVE YEARS, TWENTY FIVE FEARS

BY ERIC ORNER

2007

HOUSING EQUITY

2006

IRAQ

2005

PARENTS GETTING OLDER

2004

4 MORE YEARS

2003

DYING ALONE

TWENTY FIVE YEARS, TWENTY FIVE FEARS
BY ERIC ORNER

2002

ANTI DEPRESSANTS KILLING MY SEX DRIVE

2001

911

2000

NOT SAVING ANYTHING FOR RETIREMENT

1999

FRIENDS MORE SUCCESSFUL THAN ME

1998

WRINKLES

TWENTY FIVE YEARS, TWENTY FIVE FEARS
BY ERIC ORNER

1997

IMPEACHMENT

1996

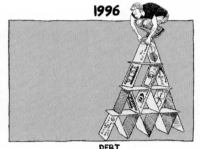

DEBT

1995

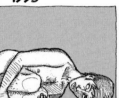

DEPRESSION

1994

ADDICTION

1993

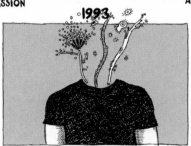

OPPORTUNISTIC INFECTION

TWENTY FIVE YEARS, TWENTY FIVE FEARS
BY ERIC ORNER

1992

STUDENT LOANS

1991

LOSING MY JOB

1990

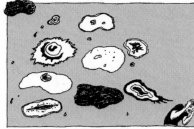

KS LESIONS

1989

TIANANMEN

1988

LOVING SOMEONE WHO DOESN'T LOVE ME

TWENTY FIVE YEARS, TWENTY FIVE FEARS

BY ERIC ORNER

1987

TEMPING

1986

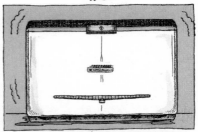

ACCIDENTALLY PICKING UP PSYCHOPATH AT BAR, WINDING UP IN HIS FREEZER.

1985

NUCLEAR CATASTROPHE

1984

MORNING IN AMERICA

1983

GAY MEN'S CANCER

CALIFORNIA

BY GEE HENRY

Gee Henry was born in Antigua, and grew up in Queens, NY. His short stories have appeared in the anthology Shade and the journal Cream Drops. He's currently working on a memoir titled The Year of the Rat. A sometime singer-songwriter, he makes a living doing publicity for books, and lives in Manhattan with his cat. www.myspace.com/geehenry

California

By Gee Henry

Michael and his Uncle Paul are visiting museums and learning many foreign and universal things. What are the limits of human suffering? How do you capture them in oils? Michael is the one who will benefit; he is twenty-three and a stranger to California, a recent transplant from New York City. Paul is seventy, a retired police officer, and has lived in this part of the world for twenty years and seen it all twice.

Michael never went to museums in New York; some people consider New York the museum capital of the world, but, really, there is plenty to observe there without going to *museums*. But Michael finds that there's not really that much to do in San Francisco other than drive over the Golden Gate Bridge into Sausalito or wait to be swallowed up by the earth. So museums it is – today they will see three of them, all in a one-mile stretch. A museum-specific guide book purchased from, of all places, a taqueria, guides the way, with pictures of exhibits and exteriors of museums. Michael doesn't know how to get around San Francisco yet, and feels like he is still a child, being taken places in the back seat of somebody's car. The exhibits blur in Michael's mind – lots of ancient statues lining marbled halls, lots of long-gone people, waving. It's all the same, thinks Michael. Paul grimaces at Michael and thinks: to be young, to be young again.

It is late summer, but everything is already cold. Rather, it's tepid in the afternoon, cold in the evening. He drove down from New York in shorts, expecting to be dark brown in no time in sunny C-A. He wanted to be completely unrecognizable, like a star. Native San Franciscans push through the streets in bombers and sweaters, completely prepared for the climate, and people have already informed him that it's L.A. or San Diego where you can get a tan, not San Francisco. He feels as though he has been made into the butt of some elaborate joke; he is still as pale as a grape.

In a museum on Steuart Street, Michael stands beneath a Bouguereau painting titled "The First Kiss," depicting a naked boy cherub kissing a vacant girl with butterfly wings on the cheek, on a cloud. Oh, God, Michael thinks, do I understand that painting. Michael's first kiss had been with Jay, who lives in New York. Michael has not seen him in three weeks, and the last time he did, Jay was shaking his head and saying that there was nothing between them. They were in an Indian restaurant, listening to a man play a dirge on the sitar. The song was a wedding song, but it was not happy or optimistic about the future. It was a song about a woman whose intended dies the day before their wedding, and who has made the decision to go ahead with the wedding and marry his corpse and be forever faithful. Of course, neither of them knew the song or its meaning, but, as Jay spoke, its last awful note was played and hung in the air, unmuted and filled with implications of sacrifice and unappeased desire. Michael held his breath for as long as the note lasted. It was on East Sixth Street, that this happened.

Michael writes in his journal: the hills are steep, very bad for driving. Cars are dying left and right here. In an overpriced diner, Paul goes over the lessons of the day as Michael pushes some wilted lettuce and tuna around his plate, listening to the sound of his uncle's voice, which is snaky and thick with fatigue. Michael wonders if he is pushing his uncle too hard. He doesn't like old people. Who does! he thinks, but does not say. His uncle folds his spectacles with a snap, like it's the principle of the matter. Michael is reading a sign over the counter. It says, welcome in to the Welcome Inn Cafe. Come say hello to Cecelia, Thursdays and Fridays from ten to two, and there is a picture of an ancient woman, propped up and beaming at you. Just below the picture is Cecelia herself, alive and kicking. It is Thursday, 1:35 p.m. He wonders why people are urged to come and see her, because she isn't doing anything special, just smiling and nodding and counting money. He figures that she must be beloved.

His uncle says, "Aren't you hungry?"

"No, sir," Michael says.

"Well, Michael, why didn't you say so? We didn't have to eat yet. The day is still young; so are we. I want us to go to Fisherman's Wharf and get on a boat and see what there is for two men to see." He lists some other things they could be doing, then waits for a reply. Cecelia, who had apparently nodded off a bit, wakes with a start. She nods smartly at Paul, then turns her gaze on Michael and shows her teeth.

Tuna accumulates in strategic mounds on Michael's plate. "Lettuce," he says.

"Hmmm?"

"Let us," Michael repeats. "Get it?"

* * *

"When I was young and would visit California, it wasn't quite so bad," Paul says at the Wharf. "It was my favorite place to go and meet my young friends, mostly boys from the Academy, like me. Now tourists come here. Tourists! Or vagabonds, selling pot." The two of them sip at beers.

I am a tourist, thinks Michael, then feels just awful. The air is very salty, because the sea is never very far away, and seems to be sucking the moisture from his face in a steady stream. He's feeling so strange, and chalks this feeling up to the beer, when it's only the afternoon, after all, and he really shouldn't be drinking. He says something to this effect out loud.

"Well especially not on an empty stomach!" Paul booms. "Man cannot live on Bud alone. Ha, ha!" He pats Michael on the back.

At night Michael smokes pot and then goes right to sleep, so it's not too bad.

* * *

He dreams, though, that he is very fat, and has driven to the supermarket for food. He leaves the motor of the car running and the keys inside, because he won't be gone for long. But then he is distracted by a dessert that's on sale. He goes over to the display and looks at the label. He opens the package and takes some, biting slowly. He could almost never control himself around anything sweet – his mother always accused him of that – but at some point during the dream, he senses that there is a stronger force within him, hidden but growing more prominent – a desire for more and more, or less and less, he can't be sure.

Suddenly, he remembers the car, still running, with the keys inside. But he can't stop eating – it's as though he has been possessed. He eats one of the desserts, then another, and another. The empty wrappers pile up on the floor of the aisle. He is eating so fast, he nearly chokes. A crowd has gathered, and watches him, and one woman whispers, "Is he going to *pay* for that?"

When he finally gets back to the parking lot, he finds that no one has stolen his car, after all. He is relieved, of course. He cannot say how much. But as he is getting inside, he finds a note, taped to the windshield.

Mister, it says. You are very fat. Please don't think me rude. I saw you as you pulled up. Please try and get some help. You are so fat.

He wakes up.

* * *

How unhappy Paul would be if Michael told him about his dreams. They don't even make any sense – he doesn't *eat* desserts. In New York, this was never a problem, because every corner had a 24-hour deli, and they all sold fruit and other dessert alternatives. If there was no deli, there would be a vegetarian restaurant. If there was no vegetarian restaurant, there would be something else. He ate with his friends. He ate with Jay. He ate by himself, whatever.

Occasionally, men he would meet in New York through his work – older men – would phone him up and ask him to dinner. He would give their offers as much silent consideration as he deemed polite. But dinner, with these men? He could barely think of it. Who wanted to eat with an old man when he had a friend, it seemed, in every neighborhood in the city. And when he had Jay. Sometimes the two of them would be eating dinner, and Michael would just start beaming like an idiot into his plate, until Jay would reach over the table and give him a good poke, just fooling around with him. There was something inside Michael then that he did not want to lose hold of.

And it wasn't like he didn't have a great deal of respect for hunger! God, he did. He was capable of real tears looking at Save the Children commercials, and would check his stomach in the mirror often to see if it was filling up with air. He was struck by the fact that there are at least two ways to get very fat – to eat a great deal, or to eat nothing at all, and let the wind take over. But he was young and careless. Sometimes he went on long camping trips, bringing only oranges or bananas or a strip of beef jerky. Although he feared hunger, he did nothing to stave it off in himself. But there were never any great consequences, nonetheless. He was never trapped in an elevator after he had skipped two meals, that sort of thing.

Once or twice he had the thought that if he was only able to eat enough of everything at one sitting, he might never be hungry again. Sometimes you read in the paper of huge men wearing bibs, like children, who ate too much of something and blew up and died. Sometimes they did it for a contest, on Coney Island. He could only eat half a sandwich before he felt like he might blow up, and certainly not the huge helpings of hot dogs or cherry pies that these men died eating. To die, on Coney Island! If he ate just two cherry pies, he would probably keel over.

The day he was to leave for San Francisco, he said goodbye to his parents. His mother was very moved, and pressed six hundred dollars into his hand. He looked into her eyes and tried to feel something other than anticipation, but he could not. The money came between them, and he U-hauled his ass out of there and across the country, keeping the hundred dollar bills under his pillow for safekeeping whenever he needed to stop in a motel for rest. Six hundred whole dollars.

Certainly, he never even imagined that, once he got to California, he might be hungry.

* * *

He meets up with his uncle again. His uncle is wearing a pair of polyester paisley pants that are too thick, really, for walking all day, and a "panama shirt" with an unusually wide collar. "We are two men, on our way," his uncle sings in a tuneless sort of way. He looks at Michael like he is trying to see how much water is left at the bottom of a well. He has brought hearty sandwiches that his aunt Poll has made. Paul and Poll, two peas in a pod.

"Now, I told your aunt that I haven't seen you eat but a morsel of food, and she sent these over. You're getting way too thin. Soon the water won't hit you in the shower." Paul laughs – that was a joke, but it wasn't funny. "Are you sure you haven't eaten something that someone might have poisoned, and that took away your appetite? Some water, some food? People can do that, you know, nowadays. There is a poison for everything. When I was still on the force, I saw a young woman who had been poisoned into thinking she was being attacked by bees. So specific! Another time, some young hotshot took too much of this or that and came in with his eyes permanently crossed. We covered the girl in blankets and called the medic. But what could we have possibly done for the boy? What, I ask you? Have you eaten anything that was just lying around?"

"No," says Michael. He can't explain it. *Nothing* could possibly satisfy him. It's all a waste. He is even trying to take smaller breaths – little sips, really – because he wants to make no impact, leave no impression. Why does his uncle have to be a retired police officer? Everything that Michael does he feels is being written down on a rap sheet. After today, he will tell his uncle not to bother meeting up with him anymore and trying to cram lessons down his throat – he can't possibly retain all this knowledge. But today they have one more museum to inspect – the SF Museum of Modern Art. There is an exhibit of Mexican art that Paul has read about and has been longing to see, featuring Frida Kahlo and her husband, what's-his-name. Michael used to like Frida Kahlo, but these days everyone likes Frida Kahlo – even his uncle, for Chrissakes! – and it's kind of embarrassing now. Frida

Kahlo is like an aunt of his who went insane and now must not be spoken of, even fondly.

They get off the elevator one floor too high and must ride back down on the escalator. Paul curses and reaches for a phantom holster. Michael notices that a woman tries to get on the escalator at the same time as himself, then takes a good look at him and chooses the stairs instead. She runs down the stairs, going faster than the escalator. It is a strange effect. They are both moving in the same direction, this woman and he, and yet she is moving away. Michael, riding quietly down, looks at her wake and wonders why he is noticing this woman at all. Who is she to be noticed? She is wearing a leotard and leg warmers, she is less than nothing at all. A woman running down the steps should be just that, nothing more. He is thinking in complete sentences and scenarios, as though he is writing everything down on a piece of paper. The woman descends to the mezzanine and disappears.

Now Michael is standing on the right floor, waiting for his uncle to finally be finished. Michael gives a perfunctory glance at a painting, thinking, What is it about Frida Kahlo that I dislike so much now. Is it her eyes? The way she seems to be glaring at you, making her own judgments? Michael stares at her arrogantly, as fiercely as being in a public place allows. What does *she* have to glare about? he thinks, suddenly upset. Frida Kahlo is wearing a braid, bright and red as a heart, in her knotted hair. The braid spills out of her hair, and he traces it with his finger. It runs down Frida's neck, breasts, and hangs coiled near her belly. It is so red, he can almost taste it in his mouth. Now, here is the part that will seem so funny to Michael later, when he thinks about it. As he looks at the painting of the braid, he begins to remember something about his life with Jay in New York. Jay used to be fascinated with the diets that Michael would go on. Sometimes he would stare open-mouthed at Michael as he ate one small carrot or a mouthful of brown rice – the only food he would allow himself for the day – watching the motion of Michael's mouth. Jay would place his hand on Michael's stomach and throat, claiming to be able to trace the path of the food as it moved through his body. His hands were so sensitive, he said, and Michael was getting so thin, Jay could even feel the progress of a pea. Nothing was more arousing to Jay than that. Michael didn't like it – that feeling of being so contemplated. For the rest of my life, he thought then, no matter where I stand or how much distance I place between myself and Jay, I will always feel as though his hands are around my neck, straining to feel something inside. Michael doesn't know why he remembers this. As Michael looks at the painting, a wave of sadness overcomes him, and his knees buckle and he begins to fall. He reaches out a hand out to steady himself, but as he does this, his uncle comes up from behind and catches him, saying "whoa." Michael tries to focus his eyes on his uncle's face, but he is crying suddenly, and can't see clearly.

Paul looks at him, alarmed. "Are you happy now?" he says, not unkindly. "This is what not eating gets you. What you're feeling is just hunger."

"Yes," Michael says. "You're right." But even that, he knows, is a lie. He is not hungry, "hunger" is a word that doesn't come close to the way he feels — he is *starving*. He eats a few bites of the sandwich that Paul brought, and then they head for a restaurant they had passed earlier, located six paces from the corner of Market and Third, five miles from Golden Gate, equidistant from Mission and Bush, travel north and turn three blocks left at the light. Michael turns the menu over and looks at the red maze of a map emblazoned on its back, saying you are here.

QUEEN OF RICE

By A. Tyler Perry

*Tyler tries to better approximate the personal-as-political,
continually inspired by the works of Lorca, Whitman,
Difranco, and Hardy. He's trained with Bent Writing
Institute, bound his poesía en Español, and attempted, in
often improvised ways, to queer syntax and grammar as
interventions into the social world. Currently his day job is
tackling the academy in pursuit of a doctoral degree.*

▼

Queen of Rice

BY A. TYLER PERRY

this is a love poem

strolling south-west down Market Street in SF,
approaching the centre of the gay universe,
met with sneers and leers from queers,

my boyfriend informed me:
"you see, baby, they see you as a rice queen."
"a wha'?"
"a white guy who only dates and fucks asian men."
"really?"

me, the supposed queen of rice
a WASP of good intentions,
wading through rice paddies of any Asian nation,
plucking up a lil' Cal Rose delight,
seductively smooth, subservient, and so passively polite.
right?

no. you see, I ain't no queen of any sort of grain.
I don't stylize my power and palate
through exoticization, tokenization, essentialization,
or any other multi-syllabic word combined with
-i-z-a-t-i-o-n.

you see, these metaphors to deny
differently lived lives
only serve to step on, stomp out, cover up
the backs, faces, limbs, artefacts
of all those who came before us,
who *somehow* made a space, a place
for difference to exist in *all* our communities.

but let's get to the real point:
our efforts to tokenize, essentialize, exoticize
simply replicate the divisive difference
that our white mono-culture needs.
you see, the beauty of whiteness is you can't behold its face.
it's a wily lil' guy, shifting, changing,
the absence – yet definition – of everything,
the standard by which all cultural clocks are set,
an imperial force for centuries now
colonizing lands, tongues, fashions, fortunes, and difference,
attempting to rape every field of its seeds
for mass consumption,
even now on the corner of Market and Castro.

so, in a word, "no."
I don't see my boyfriend, this man,
as a piece of rice to steam into submission.
given the history of my skin, the politics of my blood,
I cannot simply do him like that.
you see, he's got the genealogy imbued with
the atrocities perpetuated throughout history
by people like me,
so that when we come together
as current day lovers,
we're also the once-upon-a-time
plantation owner-and-worker
officer-and-engine man
conquistador-and-savage,
globe trotting tourist-and-infamous Makati male escort.

so I say no.
I don't see me the queen of any rice.
rather, what I see, before me,
is a man who has chosen me
worthy of *his* time, trust, and witness to a legacy.
and in the space between he and me
is a fertile ground
upon which to repair our history.

so we'll sow our seeds together,
of work, love, and justice,
repair the historical wrong
between him and me, you and we,
and we'll sow away the pain
because I cannot grow the love I have with him,
and disregard the essential pain between.
you see, this love, of all love,
has every right, need
to *now*,
at the intersection of Market and Castro,
to speak its name.

for Sherwin

LOCKER ROOM ADONIS

By Ben Barton

Ben Barton is a poet and journalist who was recently named "One of Britain's most promising young poets" by Three Lights. As well as appearing in publications such as Chroma, The Coffee House, Masque, Parameter, Poetry Monthly, Pulsar, South and X Magazine, he has also broadcast on the BBC and performed at festivals throughout Britain. His collections include The Red Book and The Hospital.

▼

Locker Room Adonis

BY BEN BARTON

Two dozen gods stood, naked
      in full stone.
I'd never been so glad
to be excluded, to just
      be among them
unnoticed.
I turned away
      and melted into the corner
not wanting to expose my dick,
      still unripe.
I never once looked directly.
Images flashed in
from my peripheral vision —
black patches, toned lines
      the nether V —
all left to my imaginings and musings
set to re-emerge in the dark.
      That boy —
he was my Zeus,
      a force of fire,
acid tongue and gargantuan cock —
      a deadly double dose.
At night I lay ready
      for him, pouring
myself out in libation,
offering him
      the sweetest part of me.

WHY HE LEFT

By Bruce Betz

Bruce Betz grew up in Louisville, Kentucky and is a graduate of Kenyon College. He lives in Seattle where he works as a marketing and travel writer.

▼

Why He Left

BY BRUCE BETZ

I can't imagine why he left.

Looking back, I think it must have been Halloween. Things took a turn for the worst on Halloween—a holiday that has never meant much to me, but did mean a lot to him. I was torn between two costumes: Catherine de Medici and Emily Dickinson. I made my decision, pulled my hair into a severe bun and slipped a drab print dress with a high collar over my head. When I walked into the kitchen, I could sense his disappointment. I think he considered Emily Dickinson a cheap shot, an easy costume. He had spent two weeks on his potted plant ensemble: His face was painted a dark brown; his head encircled with canary yellow petals, and his body encased in clay-colored cardboard pot. But to tell you the truth I think that costume caused all the trouble. I think that's why he left.

The party we went to was crowded: 40 people in a small apartment. I don't like big crowds so I decided to play the wallflower and found a quiet corner in the living room: It seemed an appropriate response given my temporary persona. Several guys asked me why I was wearing a pin that read *Ample make this bed*. During the fourth explanation, I heard a crash in the kitchen.

The wires of his costume, which held up the clay pot, had become entangled in the refrigerator David, whose clothing hung from his whitewashed body with bent coat hangers. The two of them became so enmeshed that the woman throwing the party had to borrow wire cutters from a neighbor.

Once freed, we left. In the car he told me that his side hurt and he thought we should go to the emergency room. I took the pin off my dress. I did not want to explain *Ample make this bed* to anyone in the emergency room. Well, it turned out he had a cracked rib: A potted plant with a broken stem, if you will. And the cracked rib meant he couldn't ski come November, and skiing was the thing he liked best after Halloween.

Well, to tell you the truth, sitting here in the early winter twilight, I don't miss him that much. I just wonder why he left.

JAYSON HITS THE BEACH

BY JEFF KRELL

*Jeff Krell created the groundbreaking comic strip Jayson,
which debuted in the "Philadelphia Gay News" in 1983.
By 1985 Jayson had achieved national prominence in Gay
Comix and the Meatmen series of gay male comics
anthologies. In 2005 Krell published two new retrospectives,
Jayson: Best of the 80s and Jayson: Best of the 90s. His
new graphic novel, Jayson Goes to Hollywood, will be
published in 2008.*

▼

2

3

4

FULL CIRCLE

BY MICHAEL THOMAS FORD

Michael Thomas Ford is the author of numerous books, including the novels Last Summer, Looking for It, Full Circle, Changing Tides, and What We Remember. Visit him at www.michaelthomasford.com.

Spanning nearly 60 years in the lives of two best friends, Michael Thomas Ford's novel Full Circle is also a record of the changes that took place in the gay community over six decades. The following excerpt takes place in New York in 1982, shortly after the first fundraiser was held for the fledgling Gay Men's Health Crisis, which was founded to educate the community about the growing AIDS epidemic. For more information about GMHC visit www.gmhc.org.

▼

Full Circle

By Michael Thomas Ford

The white-painted face that peered out at me from behind the door of apartment 4A looked like it belonged to a china doll. The eyes, rimmed in black, peered down demurely at the floor. The lips, red like cherries, were pursed slightly. Jet black hair was done up in an elaborate chignon pierced by ivory chopsticks. Somewhere in the room, a woman's voice soared in a moment of operatic exuberance.

"I'm sorry," I said, looking again at the number written on the paper in my hand. "I think I have the wrong number. I'm looking for John Fink."

"That's right," the woman said in a decidedly male voice. "Come in."

The door opened wider and I stepped inside. The geishalike figure, clad in a red-embroidered kimono, shuffled to the stereo and turned down the volume before addressing me again. "I'm John Fink. You must be my buddy from GMHC."

I nodded. "Ned," I told him.

John clapped his hands together, and I saw that despite the delicate kimono and makeup, his body was very much that of a man. Hairy wrists extended from the sleeves of his outfit, and the hands were much too large to be those of a woman. It was one of the signs Alan had taught me to look for when trying to determine the gender of someone who might be in drag.

"I've got lunch," I said, holding up the bag I'd picked up at the Gay Men's Health Crisis office on West 22nd Street and brought to John's apartment four blocks away.

"I'm sure it's delicious," John said as he accepted the bag from me and walked into the apartment's tiny kitchen.

I wasn't sure what I was supposed to do next. My training to be an AIDS buddy had been minimal, consisting mainly of an introduction to how they believed it could and could not be transmitted and some suggestions for handling the sometimes shocking appearance of people suffering from what until recently the medical community had called "gay cancer." In 1982, a year after the first cases had been diagnosed, there were still few definite answers about how or why so many gay men were becoming infected with this new ailment. But they were, and we were growing increasingly worried. A recent *New York Times* article--which still referred to the disease by the homo-specific acronym GRID, for gay-related immunodeficiency disease--had reported that since the first appearance of the disorder in San Francisco, at least 335 people had been diagnosed, out of which a terrifying 136 had died.

Those of us in the gay community believed that the numbers were actually much higher. In New York, we had already seen a steep rise in the number of men developing debilitating pneumonia and the telltale purple lesions of Kaposi's sarcoma. Foreseeing a health issue of epic proportions, a small group of friends had founded Gay Men's Health Crisis to gather and disseminate information as it became available. Housed in a building owned by Mel Cheren, known to most of us as the "Godfather of Disco" and partner in the famous Paradise Garage nightclub, GMHC was spearheading the movement to make gay men aware of what was happening.

In April, Alan and I had braved a freak spring snowstorm to attend the first benefit for the fledgling organization, a night of entertainment by the likes of Evelyn "Champagne" King and the New York City Gay Men's Chorus, as well as impassioned speeches asking for donations and volunteers. Moved by the occasion, and by the fact that already Alan and I knew half a dozen people from the theater community who were ill, I'd signed up to be a buddy to a person with AIDS. Now, a month later, I was making my first visit.

"Would you like me to leave you to your lunch?" I asked John as he took a plate from a cupboard and opened the containers of food I'd brought.

"I'd rather you stayed," he answered. "If you don't mind. I don't get a lot of visitors."

He sat down at the table tucked into one corner of the room. I sat across from him as he picked up a fork and began to pick at the macaroni and cheese that had been made that morning by other volunteers. I noticed that he swallowed gingerly, as if it hurt him to eat. He coughed, and the front of his kimono opened. I saw that his chest was covered with dark purple spots the size of quarters.

"The music is pretty," I said, trying not to stare.

John pulled his robe closed. "Madama Butterfly," he said. "Do you like opera?"

"I've never really listened to it," I told him. "I'm afraid I wouldn't really understand it if it's not in English."

"You don't need to understand the words," John said as he poked at a carrot. "The music tells you everything you need to know. Just listen."

He was quiet, closing his eyes as the music played. "Cio-Cio-San is a beautiful fifteen-year-old geisha," he said. "They call her 'Butterfly.' She falls in love with Pinkerton, a handsome navy lieutenant. He marries her, but he knows he can never make a life with her. They have a child. Then he leaves, promising to come back for her. She waits three years for him to return, turning down an offer of marriage from a prince who finds her beauty irresistible. When Pinkerton does come back, he brings a new wife with him. They go to Butterfly to request that she let them take her child."

John stopped speaking, sitting silently and listening to the voice coming from the speakers. I couldn't understand the words, but I could feel in the singing an intense sadness.

"Butterfly agrees to let them have the boy," said John, his voice soft beneath the singing, as if he was translating for me. "She tells them to come back later for him. When they're gone, she blindfolds her son. Then she goes behind a screen and stabs herself. When Pinkerton comes for their child, he finds her and she dies in his arms."

He was quiet again, this time for a long period during which the music swelled and filled the room. When he opened his eyes, they were wet with tears. "She loved him even when he betrayed her," he said. "And he didn't see how much he loved her until she was dying."

"Are all operas that cheerful?" I asked him.

"No," he answered. "Some are actually sad."

I laughed at his joke. He reached up and pulled the wig from his head, revealing a scalp covered in thin tufts of hair. He set the wig on the table, where it rested like a shiny cat beside his plate. John scratched his head lightly, avoiding the purple blotches that stained the skin.

"Excuse my poor manners," he said. "I realize that subjecting you to my affliction is a poor way of repaying your kindness."

"It's okay," I told him.

"May I ask why you do it?" he said.

"Do what?" I asked.

"Come here," he answered. "Visiting the dying is hardly something most people would undertake voluntarily. Usually it's done out of a sense of guilt, and I don't see that you have anything to be guilty for, at least as far as I'm concerned. We never tricked, did we? You don't look familiar, but then the lighting at the baths is not particularly illuminating."

I chuckled. "I don't think so," I said. "I guess I do it because it makes me less afraid."

"How so?" John said. "Doesn't seeing this"--he indicated his lesions--"make you fear what might happen?"

"Maybe it helps me get used to it," I suggested. "In case it does happen."

"Very practical," said John. "I commend you. And please, don't think I'm trying to scare you off. So far you are most welcome company."

"You haven't," I assured him as he resumed eating his lunch. He spilled some food on his chin, and when he wiped it away, the napkin took some of his makeup with it, revealing more lesions beneath the smooth white surface. His entire costume, I realized, was hiding the ravaged body beneath.

"What did you do?" I asked him. "Before you got . . . before." I didn't know how to phrase the question in a way that wouldn't be offensive.

"Before I became one of the damned?" he said for me. "I was a dresser. At the Metropolitan Opera. I helped people with beautiful voices get into beautiful clothes." He lifted his arm and wagged the sleeve of his kimono. "This, for instance, was worn by none other than Renata Scotto for a New Year's Eve performance in 1974. Barry Morell was Pinkerton to her Cio-Cio-San. It was divine."

"You must have seen some amazing things," I remarked.

"I have," he said. "I worked there for twenty years. It was a wonderful life. And now," he added, shrugging, "now I have the memories and the recordings."

"And the costumes," I said.

"Just a few," John said, smiling. "I don't think they'll be missed."

He finished his lunch and I cleared away the dishes for him. After that he was tired, and announced that he was going to take a nap. "But you will come back, won't you?" he asked.

"Every Tuesday and Thursday," I said.

"I look forward to it," he told me as he stretched out on the sofa in the living room. I covered him with a blanket and left him alone with his music, returning to the sunny afternoon. As I walked home, I found myself wondering if Brian had ended up looking like John at the end. I hated the idea of his handsome face being stolen from him by the cancer. I hated this disease that was feeding on the beauty of men, consuming them for some unknown reason, as if a plague had been loosed upon us. I hoped it would run its course, and soon, before too many more were taken.

That night, Alan, Taffy, and I went to Michael's Pub to hear Margaret Whiting perform. She was a favorite of Alan's, and he was particularly excited because she was singing songs made famous by Ethel Merman, whose ill-fated disco album he and Taffy sometimes performed to. As we sat at our table, waiting for the show to start, I was looking around the room when a man sitting a few tables over caught my attention. Something about him was familiar, although I couldn't place his face. Before I could ask Alan and Taffy if they knew him, Margaret Whiting came out and began singing.

Throughout the show I kept stealing glances at the man, trying to figure out where I'd seen him. It was making me crazy, because I was sure I knew him. Then, during a break between numbers, Margaret Whiting walked to his table and said, "I want to thank my husband, Jack, for encouraging me to do this show."

Instantly, I knew who he was. Jack Wrangler. I leaned over to Alan. "Did she just say her 'husband'?" I asked him.

He nodded. "I'm not sure if they're really married, but they might as well be," he answered. "They've been together a long time now."

"Does she know he's a gay porn star?" I asked.

"He doesn't do that anymore," said Alan, as if this was old news. "He makes straight ones now."

The music began again, making further discussion impossible. But I couldn't stop looking from Wrangler to Whiting. She had to be at least twenty years older than he was. And although she sang beautifully, I had a hard time understanding what the horse-hung star of <u>Raunch Ranch</u> saw in the plump, matronly songbird. When the show ended, I watched as he stood to kiss her, trying to reconcile the image of the doting lover with that of the man I'd last seen sticking it to a beefy, hairy-chested stud wearing nothing but construction boots on the set of one of Brian's films.

As I was watching them, Jack turned and looked right at me. For a moment he seemed to be thinking, then his face lit up with recognition. I was surprised to see him walk toward me, and even more surprised when he reached out to shake my hand and said, "Ned, it's been a long time. How are you?"

"I'm doing well," I answered as Taffy and Alan looked on, their mouths hanging open.

"How's Brian?" Jack asked. "I haven't talked to him in a while."

"He passed away," I told him, not sure how else to say it. "Last summer."

"Oh, God," said Jack. "I'm so sorry. I didn't know."

"It was unexpected," I said. "He had AIDS."

Jack flinched visibly. I'd heard that men from the adult film industry were running scared since the discovery that sex was a primary means of transmission of the disease, and I wondered if that had played any part in his move from gay films to heterosexual life. "What are you doing in New York?" he asked, not pressing me for details of Brian's death.

"I live here now," I answered. "I'm actually in school."

"That's great," Jack said. He took a business card out of his pocket and handed it to me. "Here's my number. You'll have to have dinner with me and Margaret one of these nights."

"I'd like that," I lied. "It's good to see you."

"You, too," said Jack. "Now don't forget to call me."

When he was out of earshot, Taffy grabbed the card from me. "I can't believe you know him," she said.

"I don't really know him," I said. "I met him a few times."

"Did you ever . . ." Taffy began to ask, looking at me and raising her overly-manicured eyebrows.

"No," I said. "I didn't."

"Too bad," said Taffy.

"You don't seem very excited about seeing him again," Alan said.

"It just reminds me of another time," I told him.

"Well, can we still go to dinner with them?" Taffy asked.

I ignored her, taking out money to pay for our drinks as Alan got up. "Come on," he said. "Let's get out of here before she asks to be in his next film."

"Oh," Taffy said, excited. "Do you think he likes Asian girls?"

We took a cab home. As Taffy talked excitedly about having seen a real live porn star, I looked out the window at the passing city. Seeing Jack Wrangler again had unnerved me, reminding me not only of Brian's death, but making me think about the unfairness of it all. Why, I wondered, were some of us dying terrible deaths while others were unscathed? Not that anyone deserved it more or less than others. Nobody deserved what was happening to us. But still, I couldn't help but question why certain men were chosen. Were we just unlucky? Had Brian's death simply been a random event? Was John's sickness merely the result of an accident? It bothered me to think so, but it bothered me even more to think that we had somehow brought this on ourselves through some action we'd believed to be harmless. All we'd ever wanted was to love one another. Now we were dying, possibly as a result.

I didn't know if I would ever have the answers to my questions or, if I did, if I would be able to live with them. I needed to believe that some things could last forever, that there was hope. I reached for Alan's hand. In the darkness, it was a lifeline to hope, and I held it, afraid to let go.

THE BROTHERHOOD

By Tyler Dorchester

Tyler Dorchester was raised on the rodeo circuit in Alberta - the Texas of Canada - and found his way out to Vancouver in 2001, where he promptly became a hippy. The Brotherhood came to him in a terrible and beautiful and strange fever-dream, and he's been trying to sweat it out ever since. The gin helps. You can follow more adventures at Brotherhoodworld.com.

▼

Intersection of Ignorance & Bliss

By Tyler Dorchester

Russian Roulette

By Tyler Dorchester

THE MUFF WALK

By Timothy State

Timothy State's blog, BalancingBoyfriends.com, has been highlighted as a "Best Gay Blog." He is a regular contributor to Chicagoist.com, as well as Swell. Most recently, Weenie Scallopini has also been accepted for an anthology, Nine Hundred & Sixty-Nine: Stories of West Hollywood, publishing date to be determined. In 2006, two of his stories were included in the Lambda Literary Award winning anthology Love, Bourbon Street. State was recognized in 2004 as one of Georgia's "Newest and Most Promising Writers" by the O, Georgia! Writers Foundation. He and his main boyfriend, Tony, now call Chicago home.

▼

The Muff Walk

By Timothy State

Taylor and Geoff have spent Thanksgiving Day apart for years now. I know this because my partner and I have spent Thanksgiving with Taylor while Geoff drives two hours to be with his parents and siblings.

Taylor has never been invited to that family table. In fact, Taylor has been intentionally uninvited to dinner and dessert and all the trimmings of a true family holiday. Taylor's presence would only be a blatant reminder Geoff has failed to find a woman. So Taylor joins Jack and Ryan, our suburban friends through whom we met Taylor and Geoff, and with whom we all spend Thanksgiving.

Geoff's not going to find a woman. The big uncooked turkey sitting in the middle of Geoff's family table is the fact that Taylor and Geoff live together. Because they love each other and are gay. His family could just serve up a big gay goose, but this would be too much to handle in their religious home.

Despite their relationship spanning decades, Geoff is welcome only if he leaves Taylor behind. This year, however, Geoff told me his family finally considered serving goose. They made it clear that they were by no means giving in to his annual pleas for tolerance. The invitation was conditional: no handholding or any other public display of affection at the table. Because that's what gays do when gathered for Thanksgiving; we French kiss before passing the cranberry sauce.

"Thank you for the invitation," Taylor told Geoff's mother on the phone. "But I've committed to cooking for the priests." Dinner was not at the rectory, but at Jack and Ryan's, where Taylor's cooking constituted maintaining a steady flow of cocktails for the clergy, my partner Tony and me, and all the other guests of Jack and Ryan, but Taylor saw no need to share these details. There was an awkward silence on the end of the phone. After all these years, it had been a stretch for her to extend the invitation, and he had turned it down. The nerve.

"Well, at least you're committed to your religion," Geoff's mother said. "I guess I admire your dedication to serve the clergy."

* * *

Shortly after marrying, Jack and his former wife bought a suburban split-level house in a subdivision called Smoke Rise. Tradition and virtue echo in the streets of Smoke Rise, where Jack and his wife set down their roots to build a family. They lived the American split-level dream, and all was wonderful—until Jack's wife left him for another woman. She took the SUV and all the power tools. He was left alone in their suburban home. With the china.

Jack stayed and eventually started dating men. One day while jogging through an urban neighborhood known for its gay gentrification, Jack bumped into Ryan. Happily ever after was a mutual sentiment and Jack and Ryan are approaching two decades filled with love and compassion and two china patterns.

There is no better occasion to put two china patterns to use than to invite their family – their chosen family – to Thanksgiving dinner. Their guests arrive shortly after noon. Ryan greets us at the door. The smell of turkey and stuffing and sweet potatoes grab us and pull us into their home. Ryan is warm and cozy in a holiday red cashmere sweater and his smile and open arms beg a welcoming hug. He takes our coats, makes any necessary introductions and points us in the direction of the self-service bar where Taylor stands, ice tongs in hand, ready to mix any concoction to delight. In the kitchen, Jack scurries around. Sporting an apron, he puts the finishing touches on a meal that has taken days to prepare. Despite the frenzy, he takes a moment for a hug and kiss.

All the guests lend a hand: stirring the gravy until it's ready, mashing the potatoes to perfection, or simply assisting with another pair of hands to lift the monster of a turkey. Guests like me, who have no skills in the kitchen—save for stunning beauty accentuated by flirtatious bursts—stand in close proximity, ready to offer our opinion on the taste of anything. Food, that is.

"That bitch is done already," exclaims Jack, his hands flailing, throwing a microburst tizzy.

"I'd always heard you were premature," I suggest.

Jack scowls at me, clearing the kitchen counter to place the early bird to rest before carving. Everything goes into double time as Ryan orchestrates the final setting of the table. Iced tea is poured, the butter set out. Salt and peppershakers are filled and placed in the center of the table.

Ryan pulls out the electric carver, and the whir of the blade sets off a tag-team relay as the food is moved from the kitchen to the basement where two dining room tables have been placed end-to-end to accommodate twenty. It's the picture-perfect family, really.

Jack stands at the head of the table, and Ryan at the other end. Former boyfriends with new boyfriends in tow, a collection of assorted friends, and a gaggle of priests line the table in between them. Whatever baggage guests may carry around, it's all been left by the front door for today. This is a family built on love and compassion. We're ahead of every child-rejecting, minister-quoting mother or father. We know how to celebrate our chosen families. We do it by combining china patterns, setting two dining room tables together and inviting all our former boyfriends to the table.

One of the priests runs into the room, a fresh cocktail in his hand.

"I think we're ready to get started," Jack says.

"Lord," the late-coming priest says as we bow our heads. "We thank you for this day, and this plentiful food prepared before us. And the companionship which we share."

We stand by the table, a circle of men holding hands. Men holding hands at the Thanksgiving table. We celebrate love and compassion with tradition and fanfare, because we do not have the luxury to take it for granted. Because we have learned that when we show love and compassion in the wrong place at the wrong time, we will be banned from our family tables, or even worse, we will end up dead in a dumpster. We have known rejection when kicked to the curb. We have known heartache when members of our community vanish into the night. How quickly the love and compassion we have to share can be taken away by another person.

"Thank you, Lord, for the family we have gathered here today, and for the family who can't be with us, whatever the reason. Grant us the wisdom to navigate the prejudice and hate that exists in our world, and the power to live truly and honestly amongst it. May we find in our hearts the love and compassion to forgive those who oppress us. Let us not forget our brothers and sisters who are not here with us today because their lives have been cut short, either through illness or through hate. For we are truly blessed to be here. Today. With each other. Amen."

We sit down.

"Which way do we pass?" I ask.

"Right!" Jack yells. "We always go right." We fill our plates with casseroles, side vegetables, salads, turkey or the vegetarian option. My partner Tony raises his glass.

"Gentlemen, I think we should have a toast." The commotion at the table quiets. Everyone reaches for his glass and raises it into the air.

"To Jack and his cooking prowess, and to Ryan for opening their home to all of us and supporting Jack and his cooking. And to family."

Our glasses clink and conversation temporarily subsides as we dive into our plates.

* * *

Wine flows freely as we recall the stories of Thanksgiving past. Conversation starts out boisterous, growing more flamboyant as couples relive the moment they met, and we all learn how there are two profound sides to each story.

"We rode the same train every morning."

"I was always running late. Normally I'd be on the earlier train."

"He sat across the aisle from me."

"You were always staring at me."

"Anyway, one day he pulled out a copy of *Finding the Boyfriend Within*."

"I bought it for a coworker."

"And that's when we first spoke. I asked him if he was having trouble finding a boyfriend."

"And I said, 'Oh, I'm in love with the boyfriend within, it's the external boyfriend I need help finding.'"

A collective coo comes from the table.

"I need more wine with this cheese," I suggest. Taylor fills my glass.

We laugh with a seminarian who tells tales of being in the military and being tarred and feathered in a hazing ritual. He had to be shaved clean.

"I'm not sure if the guys really understood how erotic it was to hold a man down while shaving his naked body," he recalled fondly. "If they had known how much I enjoyed the hazing, I probably would have been beaten to a pulp."

And for the newbies at the table, the legend of the pending post-dinner Muff Walk is told.

"We would take a walk through the neighborhood between dinner and desert," Jack explains from the head of the table, "It filled the time between a big meal and sweet desserts. Well, one year it was unseasonably cold, and there was this tragic little queen who was the boyfriend of a former boyfriend, or something." He waves his hands at the minutia of the detail. "Anyway, he went rummaging through the house looking for something warm to wear, and he found this old, old muff. My wife had left the tired old thing in the closet rotting for years.

Well, he put it on, this muff, and just pranced and flitted around the neighborhood. It was a sight. Parents came outside, gathering their children when they saw this fairy coming. After being paraded around like a queen, the muff had basically disintegrated into nothing." No one, except for our hosts, has ever seen the actual muff from which the walk draws its name.

"So where is the muff?" a newbie asks.

"I don't know what happened to that old thing. I imagine it just ended up in the trash."

We push back from the table and Taylor freshens our cocktails. One year, we ran out of cocktails halfway through an extended Muff Walk, and the following year Tony and I brought our red Radio Flyer wagon to pull the bar along, guaranteeing cocktail service for the duration.

"A good Muff Walk is long enough so that everyone runs out of cocktail just as we are returning to the house," explains Taylor, dropping an ice cube into his drink.

We make our way to the end of the driveway, and twenty slightly-spirited men spill into the street of this subdivision with no sidewalks. We move as a mass down the center of the street, our mini bar trailing like a caboose. Along the way, we admire the landscaping and the architecture, while pondering the thanksgiving unfolding inside each of these homes. Do they combine china patterns? Do they set two dining room tables together so they can invite former spouses to the table? And do they do it with the love and compassion of the cranberry sauce-passing, French-kissing gays?

This year, the impromptu parade passes along streets with no spectators. A man raking leaves in a front yard gives a reluctant wave after we all wish him well. A chocolate lab sits on a porch and watches the spectacle pass by.

* * *

A certain intimacy takes place while we stand in the middle of a suburban subdivision on a street named "Leather Stocking," and it is here that we take care of our own, as families do. This stroll is more than a time to discuss the redeeming qualities of suburban architecture and design. Dreams and aspirations have been shared while setbacks and broken promises have been put into perspective. The collective wisdom explains if you cannot get over your partner's inability to share the remote control, it is simply not going to work.

Geoff and I are trailing behind.

"I'm so glad you're here." I latch onto Geoff's arm, careful not to bump his cocktail. "I thought you'd be spending the day with your family."

"You know I'm approaching forty years old." He placed a hand along the cheek of his baby face, as if to smooth wrinkles.

"Say it ain't so! You don't look a day over thirty-eight!"

"Well aren't you kind, bitch." Geoff pats my arm. "I just decided that I was getting too old to keep playing games. I wasn't up for the drama or the rhetoric. Either my family can love me the way I am, for who I am, or they don't get to have me. So I told them I wasn't coming."

"That's very brave."

"Thank you for that, but it makes me a little sad. Anyway, I'm here, with people I love, and people who love me as I am."

PHOTOGRAPHY

By David Duchè

*Two of my great passions in life are travel and photography.
I believe that travel broadens one's view of the world. Seeing
the beauty, and sometimes ugliness, of the world has helped
me to understand that all of our lives are at once
interconnected and individual. Through my photography I
seek to document my own personal experiences, to capture
scenes and events as I see them, and to share with others the
beauty and diversity of the world I've seen. I hope my own
contributions will inspire others to do the same.*

▼

THE RAPTURE

By Jackson Lassiter

*Jackson Lassiter lives in Washington, DC with his
partner, a dog, and the devil disguised as a cat. His work
has appeared Harrington Gay Men's Literary Quarterly,
Best Gay Love Stories, Apocalypse Literary Arts
Magazine, South Loop Review, Heartland Review, Silver
Boomers, and elsewhere. Google him to read what has been
published on-line. Jackson is especially happy to appear in
an anthology that originates in his former home of Seattle.
Contact him at LuckyJRL@hotmail.com.*

▼

The Rapture

Hey gurrrl, it's Jesus, where you at? Thank God you picked up 'cause I gotta tell you what happened Sunday night. Yeah I sound different, who wouldn't? Things is different for this boy. I'm in love. Hear me? *Love.* Listen 'a this, it's real.

So Sunday me and Shiva – you remember her, that big ole drag queen thang who wears the jewel in her navel? – Sunday night me and Shiva decide to go to The Sanctuary Club. Now I wasn't looking for nothing, mind you, 'cause you know I been holed up lately, a real sad sack since that whole thing with Judas calling me out in front of everybody and everything. Two-faced jerk. I never felt so betrayed as I did at that last supper with him and all those guys and since then I just haven't felt like going out. I only went Sunday 'cause Shiva had a bad day, what with that hellion brat of hers, Vishnu, destroying the entire house. He set the drapes on fire. Did she tell you? Anyways, about nine o'clock or so, Shiva calls me at my parents' house and says she's gotta get out.

Yeah, yeah, I been staying there, staying in the basement. It's like a grave down there, a cave with no light and no air but it was kinda fitting my mood. I was feeling bleak 'cause on top of everything else I got fired from the Catholic Charities Petting Zoo. Pure jealousy: the animals liked me better than the other keepers. I can't help it; I just have a way with 'em. Simon Magus tried for three days to get the sheep to follow him, but every time I came around they all ran over to me. Baa baa baa...all running toward me like I was the good shepherd, leaving him standing there with his hands full of hay. He complained, said I didn't pull my weight when it was time to clean the manger. I tried to tell Father Francis that it wasn't my fault, that Simon Magus was just full o' sour grapes but Simon's been there since the creation and I was just the new guy so I got let go. Anyways, so I had to give up my little hole-in-the-wall apartment and move back to Mary and Joe's basement. Can you believe it? I swear, though, I'm about to rise up from that tomb. I have to git up outta there 'cause, honey, I'm in love.

So anyways, me and Shiva show up at Sanctuary and we head to the upstairs bar, you know, that one with the dance floor. Shiva asks me if I wanna little sumpin-sumpin to set the mood cause you know Shiva, she's all about the mood. But I tell her I don't need nothing cause DJ Buddha's got the place zen rockin', man. He's playing some tribal house fusion mix that's pure enlightenment. I says to Shiva *I don't need nothing, gurrrl, this music's doing it all for me.*

So we's dancing, me and Shiva, and just feeling the beats and it's all good until that creep Lucifer starts rubbing all over Shiva. You know Lucifer? Seems like that guy's everywhere. Everywhere I turn, there's Lucifer. Sure don't know his story. But that night he starts telling Shiva how if she just lets him have her goodies he's gonna keep her happy forever and she'll never want for nothing. *Never want for nothing* he keeps saying over and over again, rubbing on her butt like she's digging it or something only I can tell, she's not havin' it. Shiva, she can do way better than that creep. But he's rubbing all over her and she's tryna get away and finally she says to me *Jesus, we gotta get away from him or it's gonna get ugly. Come on, let's go downstairs.*

So we ditch Lucifer and go downstairs to that little alley, you know, that patio between the front bar and the back room where the dick dancers swing their stuff. We're standing there and the summer night air feels real nice 'cause me and Shiva, we worked up a sweat dancing and running away from Lucifer. So we's just standing there minding our own business and dissin' on all the peeps who's walking by when I saw him. Man, I saw him and I'm in love.

He was standing in that one corner, the dark one by the door where the hustlers give lap dances. He didn't look like he wanted a lap dance. Didn't look like he needed one. Looked like he needed me but he didn't know it yet. So he's standing there all six feet tall and dark curly hair and dark sexy eyes and dark stubble, just watching peeps like I was, only he isn't watching me. So I'm tossing my hair around – what you say? Yeah, I know that's cheap but sometimes these guys like my hair. They like long hair and a soft beard and linen pants and sandals. A little hippie-dippy freak gonna catch some guys for sures. So we's standing there, me and Shiva, and I'm all tryna get this guy's attention, and who should walk up to him but Zeus. Yeah, that's right, Zeus, that big ole horndog dancer with the thunderbolt tattoo on his thigh. And I can tell, he wantsa give more that a lap dance.

That's right, that ho was tryna cock block me, and I wasn't feeling it at all. I was mad, but I was nervous, too. I mean, the king of the dancers slides up to my man, now what's a little pacifist like me supposed to do? So there I am, tryna come up with my next move, and Zeus is starting his rub on this guy, and I look up and the guy is staring right over

Zeus' shoulder at me. At me! And I'm thanking God and tryna look pretty at the same time.

So this guy pushes Zeus away and walks over to me and Shiva. Pushes Zeus and his oak-sized piece away, to come to me. Don't need nothing more than that 'cause my night's made right there but then this guy just walks up and says *'sup boy? My name's Mohammed Allah, you can call me Moe.*

Moe, Moe, Moe, I'm thinking, give me Moe. I'm seeing myself writing Mrs. Moe all over everything I own, I'm seeing myself telling him right then and there that I love him and that's that. But I don't, I just say *Jesus - my name's Jesus Cristo, I'm just dancing with my friend Shiva* but when I turn to introduce them, Shiva's gone. Never saw her again the whole night. Bitch knows when to disappear.

So me and Moe's just standing there shooting the breeze and we end up talking about everything. He's telling me how he lives with his dad, Abraham, so I tell him about living in my parents' basement and all kinds of stuff and I mean, I'm telling this guy things I never told no one. That's right, not even you. I'm telling him how Mary got knocked up wit' me and the guy disappeared but Joe came along and he took us in and raised me like a son and I'm just making all this noise like this guy cares and he's making his noise right back at me and then I think *Dang, this guy does care.*

Gurrrl, I'm saying I'm in love. That's all I'm saying.

So then we start getting a little close and he's touching my back and his fingers are running under the linen and I can't help myself but I gotta feel his chest so I do and, honey, I ain't disappointed. The man's built like Plymouth Rock. Then he kisses me and I'm telling you his stubble is hella sexy on my lips and I'm like warm salt water, all kinda heavy and liquid and melting right into this guy and next thing he says *let's go somewhere a little more private.*

Yeah, dude, that's what he says. So, OK, problem. We's both staying with our parents. I mean, Mary and Joe are real supportive and they don't care who I play around with but they don't want no strangers in their house, and Moe says his dad don't really know too much and will pitch a hissy-fit if he brings some long-haired hippy chile into the apartment. Bottom line's nobody's got nothing private. So I'm all like *OK, let's at least take a walk out on the beach and make out for a while.*

So we walk out to the beach and we're tryna find a place that's kinda hidden and finally Moe finds a spot that's pretty much outta sight, just off the beach walk but behind some rushes, and the sand feels soft and clean so we lay down. First thing we see a star in the sky, brightest star I've ever seen. So Moe tells me to make a wish and I do and he wants to know what it is but I don't tell him 'cause it's him I'm wishing for. So he starts tickling me and, honey, that's when the going gets good. I'm telling you. We're kissing and rubbing and touching and kissing some more and next thing you know my linen pants are in the bushes and so are Moe's jeans. And me and Moe's rolling buck nekkid in the sand like driftwood and I can tell he wants to go for it but then I realize my butt crack is full of sand. I think, *this can't work.*

Moe, I say, *this ain't gonna happen here. I like you, a lot, and I really wanna mess around and more but this just ain't working.* And Moe looks a little sad but he gets over it kinda quick and then he makes me promise that I ain't shining him on. *You aren't shining me on?* he asks, real serious. *I've been shined on before and I don't like it.* So I kiss him, just as serious, and we lay back down and we just keep talking and kissing, kissing and talking all night long, naked on the sand under the full summer moon with the breeze rustling the rushes and the waves lapping the shore just like our tongues lapping each other.

I know, gurrrl, it's getting kinda hot over here, too.

So then just when the sun's coming up, this lesbian rent-a-cop comes along – Sergeant Helios, her name badge says – and busts us. *You boys better git up and git dressed and git home,* she says, all butch and mean like she's got the power, like she made the sun come up. Thing is, the sun was coming up and we was pretty much naked so we did what she said. So I'm shaking about a gallon of sand out of my butt and it's trickling down my pants and out the cuff and Moe's doing the same with his jeans and we're all quiet like we don't really know how to say good-bye, only I know I feel like something in the world's changed, like oil and water can mix or dogs and cats can be friends. I just feel bright and big, full of potential like the sun coming up over the Atlantic, man. I feel like some kinda divine something's opened up for me. And then Moe says to me, he says *I know it's only the first time we've been together and I'm probably breaking all the rules of hookups and dating* – he says dating, like we's already an item and then without missing a beat he keeps right on talking – *but I think I love you and I know I want to spend more time with you.* Then this angel tells me he don't wanna lose me.

I know, boyfriend, you better sit down 'cause I could hardly believe it myself. Gurrrl, this man is saying this to me. I feel like the luckiest boy on the planet. I feel like karma and fate and destiny have all rolled up to my feet in one beautiful package and I think to myself, *Moe, that ain't gonna happen, you stuck with me now.* So that's what I tell Moe. I tell him that it ain't gonna happen, that he ain't gonna lose me and that we're gonna have lots of nights and mornings and days and weeks and months and years.

Then Moe tells me he loves me again and he starts to walk away, only I remember that nobody's got anybody's digits and if I let him walk away, he's gonna lose me. And I'm gonna lose him. So I tell Moe to wait while I go find Sergeant Helios down the walk and I borrow her pen and I make Moe write down his number on the only scrap of paper I can find in the sand. You know what it was? A playing card, the two of hearts. No joke, man, the dang two of hearts.

And then I watch as Moe disappears in the rushes around a curve in the sidewalk and it looks like's he's floating down a river and just floats around the bend outta sight.

Honey, I know, you ain't gotta tell me. Right when I didn't think it was possible. What's that? Oh, yeah, gurrrl, I forgotta tell you, I got a job doing construction over at the new Nazareth Retirement Center. I'm gonna be a carpenter! My first pay check is next Friday and I already made plans to get my apartment back and then that Moe gonna catch hell. I'm telling you, I'm gonna wear that man out.

So what you been up to, gurrrl? Tell me everything.

REJOINED

By Ahimsa Timoteo Bodhrán

Ahimsa Timoteo Bodhrán's work appears in over eighty publications including Dangerous Families: Queer Writing on Surviving, Getting Bi: Voices of Bisexuals Around the World, Inclined to Speak: An Anthology of Contemporary Arab American Poetry, and Revolutionary Voices: A Multicultural Queer Youth Anthology. He encourages other queer men of color to write the stories of our lives and thanks Greg Sarris, Craig Womack, Gregory Scofield, Esera Tuaolo, Keali'i Reichel, Essex Hemphill, and Erasmo Guerra for their gifts and legacy. http://www.msu.edu/~bodhran.

▼

Rejoined

BY AHIMSA TIMOTEO BODHRÁN

when you went sober and kicked the drugs, all your
hair fell out. it's grown in, barely, but not as full. love
your smile, the way it frames your face, and the fact
you still have teeth. a few months later, what else
would you have lost? we laugh, take this moment as
gift. look for split ends.

VOICE

By Michael Carosone

Michael writes on marginalized peoples and literatures, especially people of the GLBTQ community. He completed his first book of poetry, and is working on the outlines for his novel, memoir, and collection of short stories. At various conferences, he has presented papers on queer Italian Americans. In the fall of 2008, he plans to enroll in a doctoral program in English, in which he can continue to study gender, sexuality, ethnicity, culture, and literature.

▼

Voice

BY MICHAEL CAROSONE

I have found my voice
my gay voice

it was lost for too long
but I have found it

it was hated, hushed, and harassed
hiding, held hostage
frightened and fading
oppressed and orphaned—abandoned
bullied and beaten
ignored and isolated
tortured and tormented
drowned and dying

but now it screams

LOUD

It is angry. It is vengeful.

and it is not a rainbow
not lavender, not pink
not a triangle

it is what it is
it is its own—no more apologies

and it does not have a lisp
and it does not swish
it does not sing show tunes
it does not decorate
nor does it do hair
but it can if it wishes

it will not be contained in your convenient stereotype

it is not a sinner
nor is it a saint
it doesn't believe in that religious nonsense anyway
it is not deviant/abnormal
it is not evil

it will not conform—it likes that it does not have to

it will not straighten its bend for you
it will straighten nothing for you
period

gaily, it screams
it screams it's gay

Listen. It demands to be heard.

URBAN VELVET

By Mark Andrews

Mark Andrews is a lifelong comic book fan; he currently has an ongoing story called "Love, Death & Ufo's" being published online at PrismComics.com, and has been previously published in the 2007 Prism anthology with his new work called "Urban Velvet" (urbanvelvetcomic.com).

▼

Urban Velvet

By Mark Andrews

ABOUT GAY CITY HEALTH PROJECT

Gay City Health Project is an innovative multicultural gay men's health organization located in Seattle, WA. Built by community members in 1993 to radically change gay communities and cultures in Seattle, Gay

City gained its 501 (c)3 status in 1995. Our mission is to promote the health of gay and bisexual men and prevent HIV transmission by building community, fostering communication, and nurturing self-esteem.

Our approach to gay and bi men's health begins with the idea that we are our own best teachers. Bringing men together to talk about the substance of our lives through activities like forums, special events, groups, workshops, and health services allows for deeper interactions where we can learn from and support one another.

Why a literary anthology?

Notions of representation and identification are an important aspect of *Gay City: Volume One.* The arts allow LGBT people to see their stories and lives portrayed, and also to experience the feeling that others "get it" – the sense that other people also recognize queer moments in literary and visual arts.

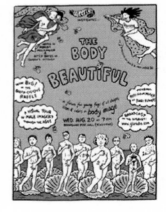

From a health perspective, this shared sense of identity and community helps to eliminate loneliness and isolation, feelings that often lead to unhealthy behaviors. The arts can give people a voice that may otherwise not be heard in today's society, and provide an outlet

to those who might be afraid to speak up. This is a valuable tool for marginalized populations. The chance to record thoughts, fears, and dreams is a chance to be seen, to be heard, and to be understood.

Gay City: Volume One is one of several projects at Gay City that seek to use the arts as an innovative medium to explore difficult health and community issues. With *Speed, Sex, and Sanity*, spoken word, film, painting, and theatre production have been employed to allow gay men to explore their relationship to crystal meth and to one another. Our arts efforts also employ technology, with the launch of *Gay City TV*. GCTV is an innovative digital media and film project that uses the internet & event-based digital recording to bring ideas and people together.

Gay City's community of men and women repeatedly express that using the arts gives them a critical distance that allows them to speak honestly and fully, and express themselves differently than just having conversations with their friends. We are eager to continue exploring issues of gay men's health and wellness in these innovative and exciting ways.

How you can help

As a community, we take care of each other by volunteering our time, supporting healthy behaviors among our friends, and contributing financially to organizations like Gay City. Your donations ensure that everyone seeking help from Gay City can receive it.

At a time like this, it is imperative to strengthen health and wellness services for gay & bi men. Our community has a history of supporting healthy lifestyles, and even with today's challenges, we can continue to build healthy communities.

You have the power to make an impact. You have the ability to influence the health and future of the gay community by making a contribution to Gay City Health Project.

You can donate online at www.gaycity.org, or send your contributions to

Gay City Health Project
511 E Pike Street
Seattle, WA 98122

Gay City Health Project History

1993

A group of local AIDS educators and community activists forms the MSM (men who have sex with men) HIV/AIDS Prevention Task Force. The group charges itself with assessing AIDS education efforts targeted at gay and bisexual men. Men who have sex with men accounted for 90% of all new infections, but only 20% of locally distributed HIV Prevention funds were targeted toward meeting their needs. Alarmed by this inequity, the Task Force makes independent recommendations to the King County HIV/AIDS Planning Council.

1994

In January, the MSM Task Force presents "Why Are Fags Still Fucking Without Condoms?" This public forum draws over 300 men, who speak of grief, loss, depression, survivor guilt and disconnection from the community. Men express how prevention tactics failed to address their concerns. The community sent a clear message: educators must work harder to reach those most at risk for HIV infection.

The MSM Task Force changes its name to Gay Men's AIDS Prevention Task Force (GayMAP) and holds three more forums in 1994. Attendance grows at each forum and the voices grow stronger. Public Health Officials can no longer ignore the need for new HIV prevention strategies for gay and bisexual men.

1995

Gay City Health Project is founded in April with a grant from Public Health - Seattle & King County. Dedicated to bold, innovative programming, Gay City continues GayMAP's provocative forums and expands to include a variety of groups, workshops and other educational and community events.

Gay City employs the concept of social marketing to get out its community mobilization and empowerment message. By using business sector marketing strategies, Gay City is able to engage the community like never before.

1996

The Greater Seattle Business Association recognizes Gay City as Non-Profit of the Year.

In April, Gay City starts Queercore, a program for guys under 30 that addresses the unique concerns of being the second generation of gay and bi guys affected by the AIDS epidemic.

1997

Gay City receives a three-year $500,000 grant from the Centers for Disease Control and Prevention to continue and expand its creative programming. By this time, nearly a hundred organizations throughout the world have developed programs based on the Gay City model, making Gay City part of a larger movement of holistic approaches to gay and bi men's health.

In response to combination therapy and the success many were experiencing with new treatment options, Gay City hosts "The End of AIDS: Hope or Hype?"

1998

Gay City makes a major impact with the launch our media campaign "We're All In Bed Together". The campaign seeks to raise awareness and increase community dialogue about our individual and community-wide roles in HIV and STD prevention.

Gay City presents the popular community forum "The Great Age Divide," initiating broad conversation about the need for cross-generational dialog.

1999

To better address the concerns and issues of first generation AIDS survivors, Gay City starts the Over 40s Project in collaboration with Seattle AIDS Support Group.

2000

Gay City Health Project begins branching out from strictly HIV and AIDS issues in 2000. Party Smart is a media campaign designed to address substance use in the community with hard-hitting messages presented in a non-shaming and non-judgmental way.

Gay City University, which provides opportunities for growth and learning through non-graded courses, wins a "Best of Seattle" Award from Seattle Weekly.

Gay City works with Public Health in crafting an innovative Hepatitis vaccine education campaign.

Gay City presents "Pride and Prejudice" to a packed house and initiates an intense conversation about race in the gay community.

2001

King County Tobacco Council presents their Ostrich Award for "getting people's head out of the sand" to Gay City's *Out to Quit* campaign. The campaign receives numerous other accolades from queer health groups across the nation.

Gay City collaborates with Toys In Babeland in presenting "Suck My Gender", an eye-opening community forum focusing on the complexities of gender and sexuality.

Gay City presents "Fear My Love," a provocative discussion on HIV Status and Intimacy.

2002

Referring to us as a "heroic local group," Seattle Weekly names Gay City one of Seattle's Dozen Rays of Hope in 2002, a spotlight we shared with groups such as the Children's Alliance and Washington Alliance for Immigrant and Refugee Justice.

Gay City initiates Crew, an all-ages volunteer group committed to creating community building and health initiatives. Some of the first programming includes Yoga and CookBoys.

Gay City collaborates with The Northwest Network in presenting "Domestic Disturbance", a groundbreaking community forum about male-on-male domestic violence.

2003

Gay City brings then Executive Director of the National Gay & Lesbian Task Force Lorri L. Jean to speak on the current and future state of queer activism.

Gay City produces ACTION: a handy STD guide for gay, bi & trans men, also making it available online.

Gay City brings over 400 community members and allies together, along with 17 partner organizations, in a series of three public forums about HIV and STD rates among gay and bisexual men in King County.

Gay City receives its first research dollars for "The Sex Check," a collaborative project with the UW School of Social Work.

Gay City launches a new grassroots media campaign and website - DemandHealth.org.

2004

To aggressively address the need for expanded community-based and accessible testing services, Gay City Health Project Wellness Center opens on February 3rd. Gay City begins providing the community access to the latest HIV and STD testing technologies in an inviting and welcoming community space. Opening the Wellness Center triples the availability of community-based HIV and STD testing in Seattle.

Gay City hosts "Tweaked: A Community Forum for gay, bi and trans men about the Highs and Lows of Crystal Meth," initiating meaningful dialogue about how crystal meth is impacting our communities.

In addition, in partnership with the local Gay Men and Drug Use Workgroup, Gay City publishes "Deconstructing Tina," a resource guide on crystal meth in gay communities.

Gay City launches Healthy Penis, a media campaign to get people tested for syphilis.

2005

Gay City significantly expands our ability to serve the needs of gay and bi Latinos through an expanded partnership with Entre Hermanos, Seattle's LGBT Latino organization. Entre Hermanos moves into our offices at Broadway and Pike.

Gay City partners with the University of Minnesota on our second research project, "Positive Connections."

In partnership with Verbena, Gay City expands our role on the Cross Cultural Health Coalition, working to address health disparities across Washington State.

Gay City hosts "The Future of HIV Prevention" initiating meaningful dialogue about where HIV prevention is heading, what questions remain relevant to gay men, and connecting some of the leading behavioral and biomedical researchers directly to community voices.

2006

Gay City and Verbena launch the Center for LGBT Health, bringing two well-established, longstanding nonprofit organizations dedicated to LGBT health into one facility. In partnership with Kaladi Brothers Coffee, we open a full service coffee house within the space to provide a meeting place for individuals and a perfect home for evening community gatherings.

Gay City and Verbena are given the Community Spotlight distinction at the annual HRC dinner in Seattle for our work on the Center for LGBT Health and are awarded the "Apples and Oranges" award for community collaboration at the Fruit Bowl Awards, hosted by the Seattle LGBT Community Center. We are also named Grand Marshall of the Pride Parade.

Gay City expands our outreach testing, providing HIV testing and counseling on a regular basis at Sea-Mar Community Health Center, the Mexican Consulate, Consejo Counseling & Referral, Casa Latina, and at South Seattle Community College.

Gay City launches "Partners for Health," a new annual giving program.

Gay City expands our work on crystal meth in partnership with Project NEON, creating "Speed Sex and Sanity." The innovative program explores the relationship gay men have to crystal meth through the arts, and is recognized for its innovation at the 2007 National LGBTI Health Summit in Philadelphia.

2007

Our tobacco work takes on a new political edge and the new strategy results in improved outcomes, with 75% of participants in our smoking groups remaining smoke free six months after their quit date.

Gay City University moves to a new location, the Northwest School, and we are introduced to a whole new generation of gay and queer young people.

Gay City expands out outreach HIV testing, adding a site at POCAAN, the People of Color Against AIDS Network. In addition, we enter into an exciting collaboration with the Center for Multicultural Health to provide testing to local African Immigrants, a community particularly hard hit by HIV.

Gay City joins with other local activists to host monthly discussions of safety issues on Capitol Hill after a series of gay bashings. We bring nearly 300 concerned community members and business owners together for a forum with the police, local lawmakers and prosecutors.

2008

Gay City launches *Gay City TV*, an innovative digital media and film project that uses the internet & event-based digital recording to bring ideas and people together.

Gay City is part of a Peer Recovery Network that receives federal funding to reduce stigma and build connections among LGBT people in recovery and the larger community.

The queer anthology GAY CITY: VOLUME ONE provides a creative forum for previously unpublished comic art, fiction, poetry, and photography that serve to promote Gay City's mission.

Gay City is named to host the National Gay Men's Health Summit in Seattle.

Editors

Jeff Crandall:

Jeff is a Seattle poet, glass artist and a founding editor of Floating Bridge Press. His work has appeared previously in *Beloit Poetry Journal, Bloom, Cream City Review, JAMA, Mudfish,* and *Seattle Review* among others. His manuscript "Clear Cut" was a finalist for the National Poetry Series. His book of poems, *The Grief Pool* is published by Firestorm Press.

J.A. Deveaux:

J.A. works as a grant writer for a literary arts nonprofit organization, and flies by night as an amateur trapeze and aerial rope artist. He also writes fiction. His stories have appeared in *Marion Zimmer Bradley's Fantasy Magazine, when it rains from the ground up,* and *Best Gay Love Stories 2005.* His next story, *"Learning to Roll My R's"*, is forthcoming in Spring 2008, in *Between the Palms, Volume II.*

Vincent Kovar:

Vincent's work has appeared in journals like *The Oregon Literary Review, Ellipsis Magazine, Thuglit* and *The Blithe House Quarterly* as well as dozens of other periodicals like *Pride Magazine, The Southern Voice, Watermark, Texas Triangle* and on *PlanetOut.com.* He is currently a contributing writer/editor for *'mo Magazine* and an adjunct professor at the University of Phoenix.

Michael Lehman:

A graduate of the University of Kansas and the William Allen White School of Journalism and Mass Communications, Michael serves as the editor-in-chief of *'mo Magazine* in Seattle, WA. His goal with the *Gay City Anthology* is to promote a broad range of talent and perspective from within the LGBTQ community. A rural Kansas boy at heart, Michael is finding his way in life and in the big city with the love and support of his brilliant and beautiful partner, Peter.

Malcolm Smith:

Malcolm Smith's photographs have appeared in publications around Seattle, including *Seattle Magazine, The Stranger* and *'mo Magazine,* as well as various CD covers, calendars, and websites. He also donates his services to local nonprofit groups such as the Human Rights Campaign, Gilda's Club, Equal Rights Washington and Multifaith Works. Photography clients include The Production Network, Microsoft, *The Stranger,* Gray Line of Seattle, *425 Magazine* and many more.

moseattle.com

'mo

™

M A G A Z I N E

is proud to support

Gay City: Volume One

celebrating Seattle's
gay community